Grave Marker Symbols

A Field Guide

To John. Rest in Peace. Michael Zahs.

Loren N. Horton
Michael D. Zahs

PBL Limited
Ottumwa Iowa

GRAVE MARKER SYMBOLS: A Field Guide

This edition published 2018

10 9 8 7 6 5 4 3 2 1

ISBN: 1892689758
ISBN 13: 9781892689757

Printed in the United States of America

Photography: Copyright John Richard, Loren N. Horton, Michael D. Zahs, Michael W. Lemberger, State Historical Society of Iowa. Used with permission.

Bible quotations: King James; Revised Standard; New International.

Rights Editor
PBL Limited
P.O. Box 935
Ottumwa IA 52501-0935

Visit our website at www.pbllimited.com for more information about this and other publications. Quantity and wholesale prices are available.

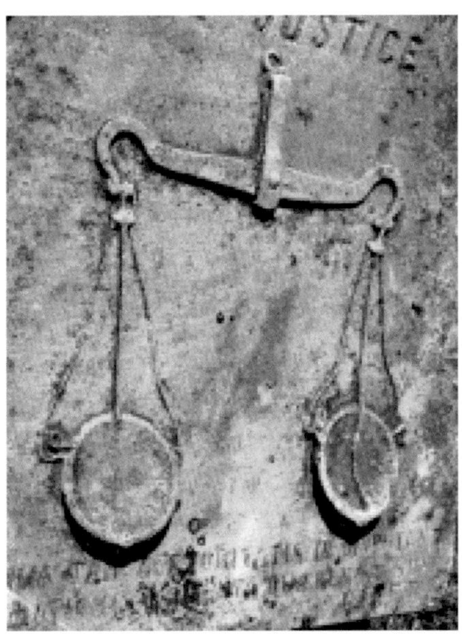

DEDICATION

BY LOREN N. HORTON

This book is dedicated to Iva Verona Brooks Horton and John Samuel Horton, my parents. Their frequent visits to the family grave yards during my childhood encouraged my early interests in the grave makers, and in the beauty and the elegance of the symbols found on them. Our annual trips to these grave yards on Decoration Day were events to which I looked forward each spring. Thank you for cultivating my love of history.

BY MICHAEL D. ZAHS

This book is dedicated to my grandmother, Marie Skubal Whetstine, and my mother, Elaine Whetstine Zahs. We always visited cemeteries on Decoration Day and at other times. It was very important to them and became important to me. This book also is dedicated to all of my students who went on hundreds of cemetery tours.

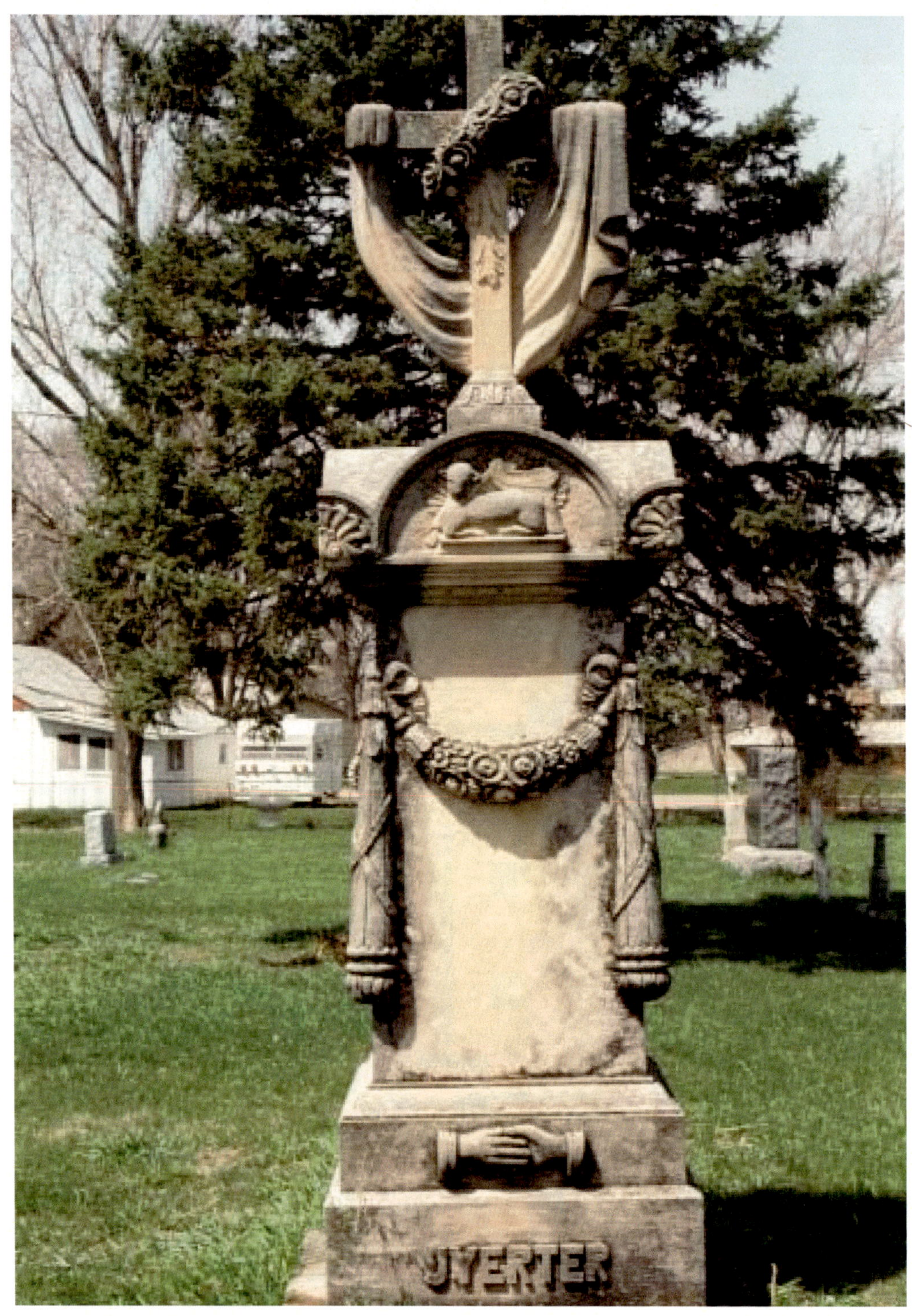

CONTENTS

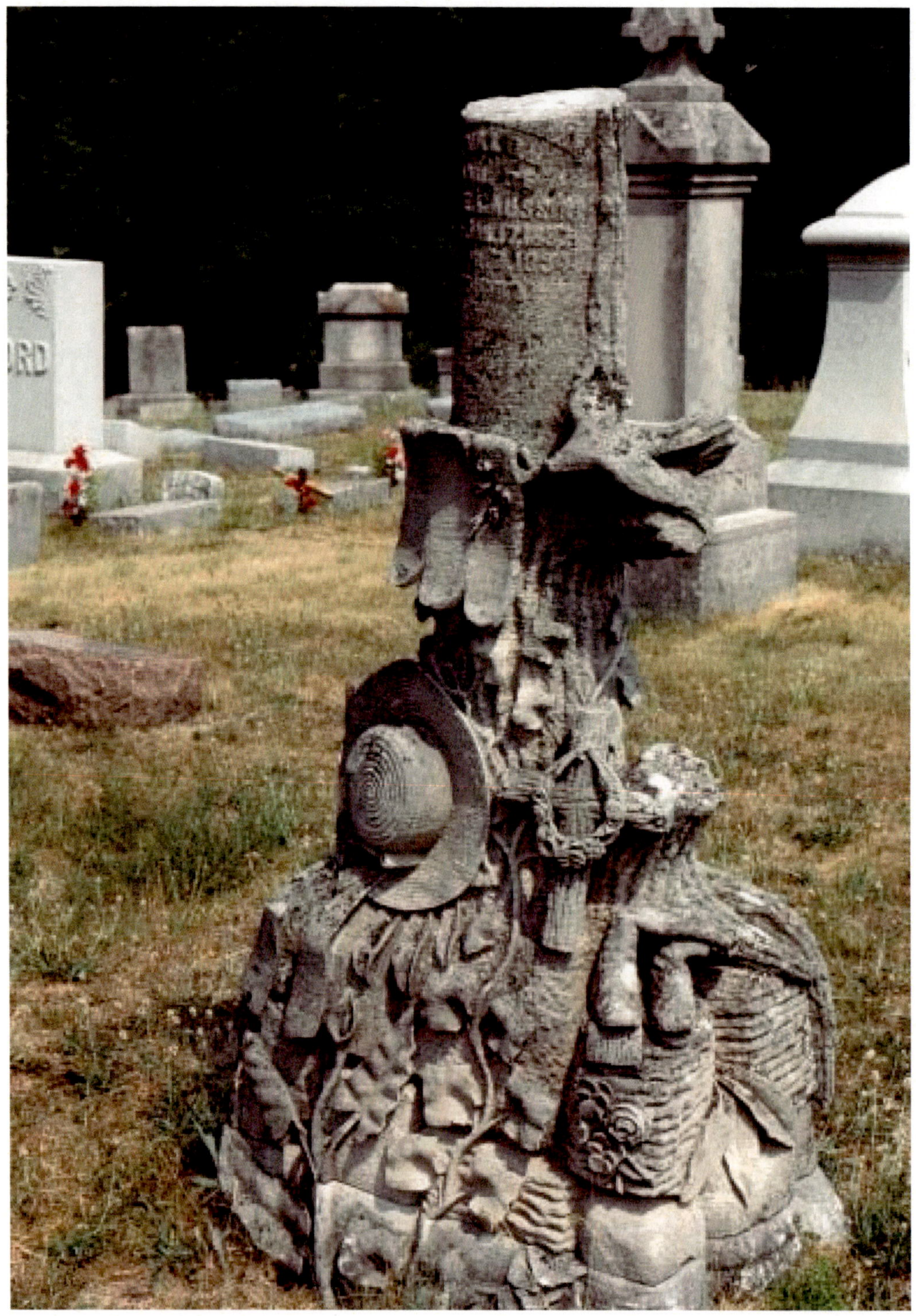

"It is almost certain that vocal language in humans first evolved as a supplement to gestural forms of communication. Indeed, even now most of us instinctively resort to gesture, both when we cannot find the right words to express a thought and when we wish to dramatize or emphasize words we use. And when someone asks for directions, we nearly always respond by pointing, to supplement our verbal reply. . . . It is remarkable how people, however articular (sic), will unconsciously resort to hand movements when the right words do not come to mind. Not further that we common speak of the sum total of a person's physical movements, intended or involuntary, as 'body language'."

--Lloyd Geering, *From the Big Bang to God: Our Awe-Inspiring Journey of Evolution*. Salem, Oregon: Polebridge Press, 2013, p. 68.

"Symbols surround us every minute of the day – and many reach out and grab us, begging us to notice them and tap into the rich wisdom they hold in store."

--Bonnie Bright, "Psyche and the Symbolic Life: How Do Symbols Transform You", *Depth Psychology*, (5 May 2012), p. 10.

"By paying attention to symbols, we can gain access to a new realm that brings balance to our conscious view, rather than a mere reiteration of what we already know."

--Morton Kelsey, *Dreams: A Way to Listen to God*. New York/Mahwah, New Jersey: Paulist Press, 1978, 1988, p. 32.

INTRODUCTION

Ever since human beings have lived on earth, human beings have died on earth. Where there are deaths, there also are a myriad of methods of disposal of the remains of deceased persons. In some cultures there is the perceived need to mark the place of disposal, perhaps even to create a memorial to the deceased person. The materials used to create such markers, the size of the markers, and the inclusion of ornamentation on the markers can be helpful in the identification of the deceased.

During primitive eras, no doubt, the materials used for such markers were those to be found locally. Such materials might or might not be of the type to last a long time. Some cultures saw the need for so-called "permanent" markers. On the other hand, some cultures might deliberately create markers that would disappear over time.

Climate always has been an issue. Some materials deteriorate more rapidly in warm, wet climates. Other materials deteriorate because of strain from freeze-thaw cycles. Only in very hot, dry climates was it possible to use wood and expect it to last for many years. All of these factors presumably were recognized by people throughout history.

Longer-lasting grave markers are a means of understanding the lives of the people who created them, as well as the life of the person whose grave is marked.

Improved technology brought an increased ability to create designs and other means of communication on grave markers. These improvements allowed the use of materials that formerly had been too difficult to carve or shape. Formerly softer stones and softer woods were used by default. Not until the latter decades of the 19th century did technology permit regular use of granite stones as grave markers. Granite is simply too hard a substance to yield easily to a stone mason's mallet and chisel. During the same era, metals that quickly corroded were replaced by metals treated to delay or to eliminate corrosion.

During the 19th, 20th, and 21st centuries, more exotic materials also came into use for creating grave markers. These included such materials as fired clay, metal alloys, concrete, and in more recent years, plastics. Cultural norms, availability of materials, craft skills, religious beliefs, and costs are all factors in the story of the marking of graves and the creation of memorials to the deceased.

When grave markers exist, there must also have been craftsmen to create these markers. Stone carvers, carpenters, and other skilled men and women had to be available to make the headstones, the footstones, and other objects used to identify a grave, and to identify the person who was buried in the grave.

Since the majority of grave markers traditionally have been made of stone, it is appropriate to discuss stone masons. Famous stone buildings have been constructed in ancient times, classical times, and the centuries since then. Also, beautiful stone grave markers and memorials have been created during the same historical periods. From the pyramids of Egypt, to the sarcophagi of European kings and bishops, to the Taj Mahal, to the tombs of "Unknown Soldiers," many examples of these stone memorials exist today. Often these stone edifices are ornamented, both with symbolic and with representational artwork. In some cultures it has been common to create effigies of the deceased, often to denote the social or political position of the person buried or entombed there.

Although some ornamental carving simply was for beauty, other figures and embellishments on grave markers and tombs were more utilitarian. Names, ranks, birth and death dates, and family relationships might be included. Even the placement of the grave or the tomb, within a church or within a churchyard cemetery, may give clear indications of the ranks, titles, and social importance of the families of the deceased persons.

It is likely that the very first communication between and among human beings may have been either gestures or some sort of vocalization. Perhaps at first it was a combination of body language and sounds. No one really knows. As societies became more complex, true speech was developed, and then later the markings that we call an alphabet came about. But writing often was the prerogative of an elite class. Ordinary, common people mastered speech, but far fewer of them were literate in the sense of having the skills of reading and writing.

Because of this lack of literacy skills, the language of communication by symbols was developed. A symbol may be defined as a mark, a sign, or a picture that indicates or is understood to represent an idea, an object, a feeling, or a relationship.

Although much communication is achieved through the use of symbols, when language is based upon commonly understood letters or words, it is not necessary to characterize written language as symbols. The symbols relating to grave markers and tombs often take the form of visual and artistic images. These visual images are intended to convey other ideas or beliefs.

The word "symbol" derives from the Greek "symbolon," meaning "token" or "watchword." It is an amalgam of "syn", meaning "together," and "bole", meaning "a throwing or casting." The sense in the evolution from Greek is a transition from "throwing things together" to meaning a token which helps to determine an outward sign of something else. A symbol really means *something that stands for something else*. When the meaning of the original is commonly understood, then the meaning of the symbol is clear.

Thus a person who cannot read or write can still understand the meaning of

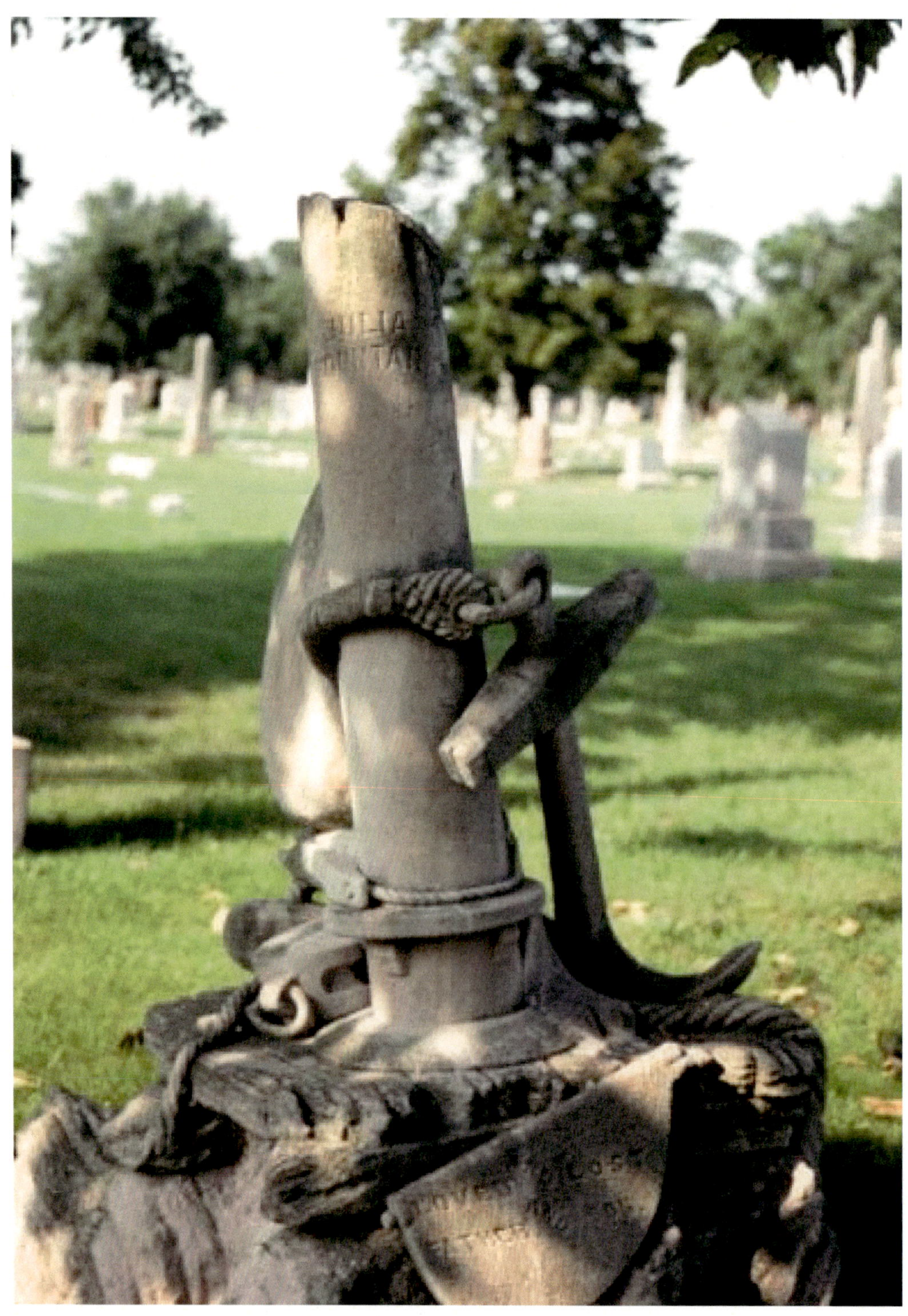

symbols. Such a person might know the significance of the three balls over a pawnshop door, or a striped pole in front of a barber shop. Pubs in England used to be recognized by objects which indicated that they sold ale. Illiterate people readily learn what service or product can be obtained in such locations.

Symbols are powerful and effective means of communication. However, the definition of what a symbol really means is only as effective as the extent to which the common meaning is generally accepted. Such common meanings may be restricted to a narrow geographic area, or to a particular cultural, ethnic, or linguistic group of people. A symbol may have other limitations as well. The same symbol may have different meanings, depending upon time and place of use. Sometimes alternative meanings of symbols might be pejorative. Whenever anyone states that a particular symbol "means" such and such, the understanding needs to be that such a "meaning" is what that symbol "means" to a special group of people, or to the people in a special geographic area, or to the people who live in a specific time period.

The universality of symbols is somewhat limited, much like the true understanding of colloquial speech, which is limited to those who have learned the hidden nuances. In 20th and 21st century advertising (print, broadcast, or visual media) viewers quickly come to associate certain products or services with certain symbols. However, what may be understood in one country may be a complete mystery to the people in another country. Only very few symbols have universal application. Many of these universal symbols have to do with dangers, with traffic, or with other restrictions. For instance, the Vienna Convention on Road Traffic, in 1968, standardized international traffic laws. More than 65 nations are signatories to this agreement, leading to the common acceptance of symbols relating to traffic movement.

Symbols frequently are used on grave markers and tombs. These symbols may be interpreted in a general way, or a specific symbol might focus on individual traits. Whatever the case, the symbols on grave markers can be extremely helpful in understanding about the time, the place, and the culture of the area in which the burial took place. This usually leads to generalizations about the symbols used on the graves of the majority of the persons buried in that time, place, and culture. Of course we must not expect that a symbol in China will necessarily mean the same thing as that same symbol in Norway. Languages, cultures, traditions, geography, and time are all factors that may lead to different definitions.

For example, the swastika cross is identified instantly by many people as the symbol of the Nazi Party in Germany from 1933 to 1945. But the swastika cross also is a common symbol in Navajo rug weaving, and it also is found in the visual arts of many other cultures throughout history.

Nevertheless, it is always useful to examine the symbols on grave markers and tombs, and to make attempts to understand what these symbols meant to the people at the time and the place that the burial occurred.

In this study we will concentrate on symbols commonly used in the United States, particularly in the Midwestern region. Most of the symbols illustrated and interpreted here were in use during the 19th and 20th centuries. Because the vast majority of the people who died and were buried in the graves which will be examined were Christian, the definitions of the symbols will rely heavily on the Christian interpretation. While there often is a much more ancient tradition behind the meaning of a Christian symbol, that tradition may or may not have been known to the people who chose a particular symbol for the grave marker of a deceased family member.

This is the reason for the large number of biblical references to the meanings of many of the symbols listed.

****

Many people visit cemeteries. Often the occasion for the visit is to attend the funeral or the burial of a relative, a friend, or a neighbor. Some people also visit cemeteries on Memorial (Decoration) Day, to pay respects at the graves of deceased family members. Other people may visit cemeteries to determine or check names and dates for genealogical information. People also visit cemeteries to admire and enjoy the artwork, the vegetation, and the landscaping.

In the time before public parks, grave yards were used for social and recreational purposes. Families gathered near the grave sites of relatives for picnics and other social occasions. All of these are the common and the legitimate reasons for visiting cemeteries.

But cemeteries and grave markers have many other things to tell a visitor. Most graves are identified by markers, which are made from a variety of materials. Grave markers are created in a myriad of sizes, shapes, and colors. They contain an equally diverse amount of information. If we observe carefully, grave markers can tell us many things.

1. **The names.** This may suggest the ethnicity of a family, and even of a community, and it may help to identify family relationships and groups.

2. **The dates.** There may only be the years of birth and death. Sometimes the dates indicate the age of the person buried in this grave. The age may be given as "died, aged 56 years, 8 months, and 10 days." Specific and complete birth and death dates might be included. The dates might be given as "born 14 July 1872, died 26 October 1932". Ages of persons at death that are unusually young or unusually old give clues about health and medical situations at the place and time.

3. **Other words and phrases.** The place of birth and/or death may be included. The cause of death may be mentioned. There may be an epitaph or an expression listed. This

might be a Bible verse, a stanza from a favorite poem, a motto, an occupation, or (in some cases) a humorous reference. A grave marker might contain such words as "he has slipped the surly bonds of earth." Words on grave markers are most often in English, but they might be in another language, which is another clue to the ethnicity of the deceased. Words on a grave marker give us added insights into the personality of the deceased person.

4. **The lettering.** There are many possible styles of lettering that can be carved on a grave marker. Lettering may be incised, or it may be in relief. The cost of the marker often depended upon the number of letters and numbers carved on it, and any use of different styles of lettering increased the cost. A variety of typefaces may be used, and different lettering fonts may appear on the same grave marker.

5. **The materials.** A grave marker can be made from a variety of different materials, and sometime different materials are used on the same grave marker. Some materials may be available locally, but some needed to be brought in from a distance, sometimes a considerable distance. The choice of material might have been determined by cost, or by the fashion of the time and place, or sometimes simply by availability.

6. **The identification.** Some grave markers display the name of the stone carver, the monument dealer, or the monument manufacturer.

7. **The symbols.** Dozens of different symbols have been used on grave markers. A symbol may have had a common meaning, understood by most of the people who lived at the same time and place as the deceased. But symbols also may have a specific individual meaning, applying only to the person buried in this particular grave. Additional information about symbols and their probable meanings will be found in other sections of this book.

Once a grave marker has been examined for size, shape, color, and materials used, it needs to be examined additionally for name(s), date(s), other words, lettering styles, and symbols. Always examine the entire marker. Look at all sides, the top, and base. All of these factors may contain helpful information.

Throughout this introduction the term "grave marker" has been used to describe the object which identifies the person buried in a particular grave. Common use of the term "tomb stone" is misleading, because (1) A tomb is an above-ground disposal of the remains; a grave is the below-ground disposal of the remains. (2) The object which identifies the person buried in this particular grave may be stone, but also it may be made of metal, wood, plastic, cement, or other materials. For these reasons, we will refer to the object identifying the person buried in any particular grave as a "grave marker." It is an all-inclusive term that includes all type of materials.

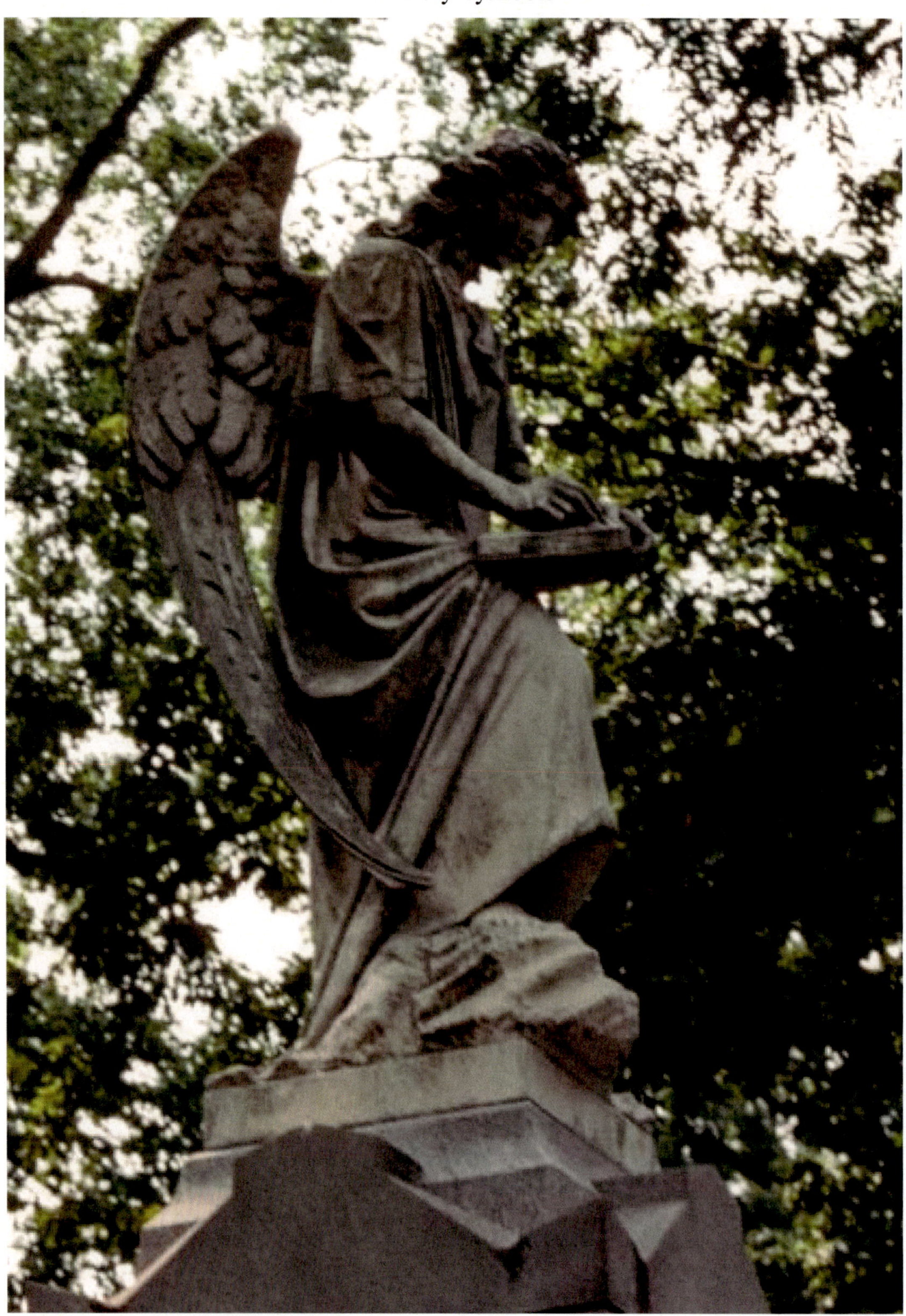

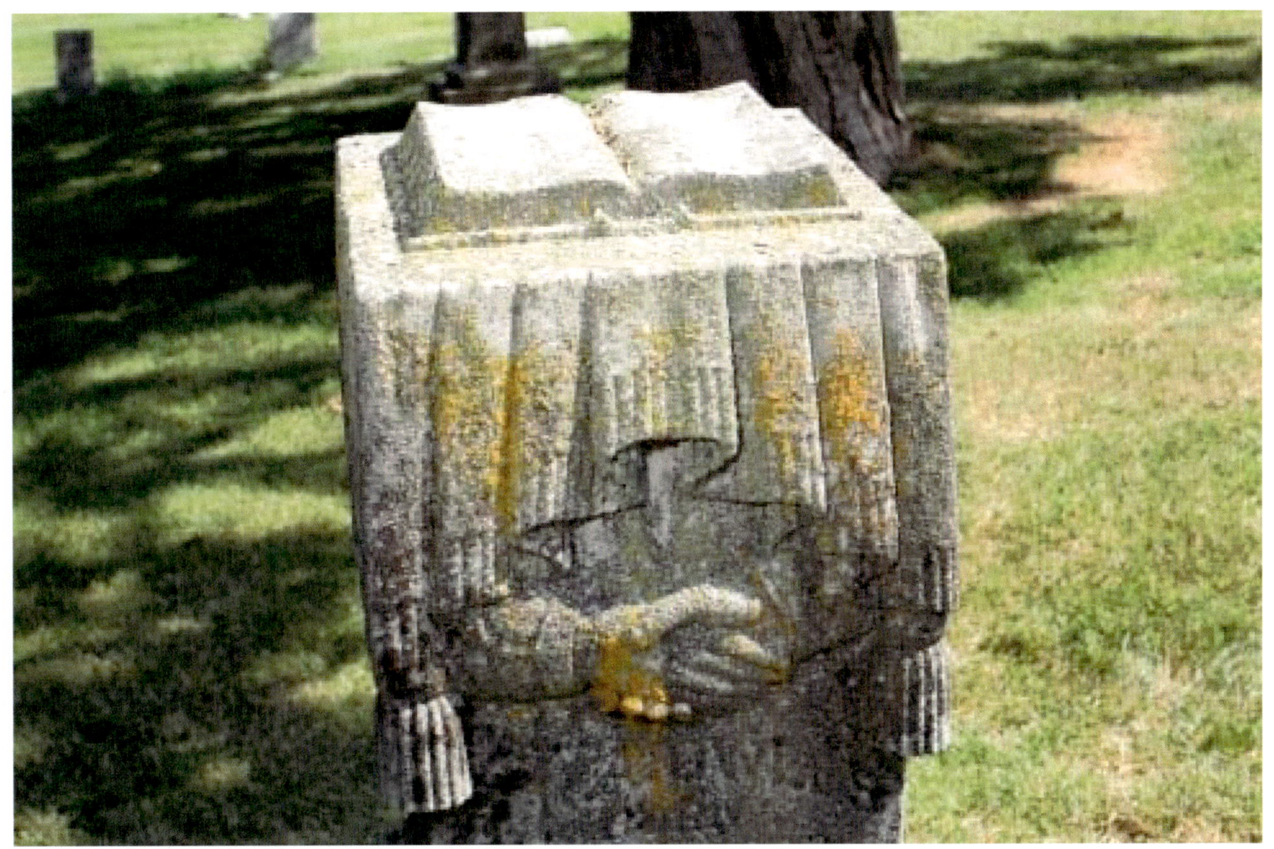

GRAVE MARKER SYMBOLS

Several of the symbols commonly found on grave markers are also symbols used by the Masonic order and other fraternal lodges. Since it is often not possible to determine whether or not the deceased person was a member of such an organization, we will not attribute the organizational meaning to any symbol unless it clearly is appropriate.

The complexity and the delicacy of symbols on grave markers depended, at least partially, on the availability of suitable materials. But these factors also depended upon the availability and the skills of local craftsmen. Both of these factors were as important, if not more important, than contemporary styles.

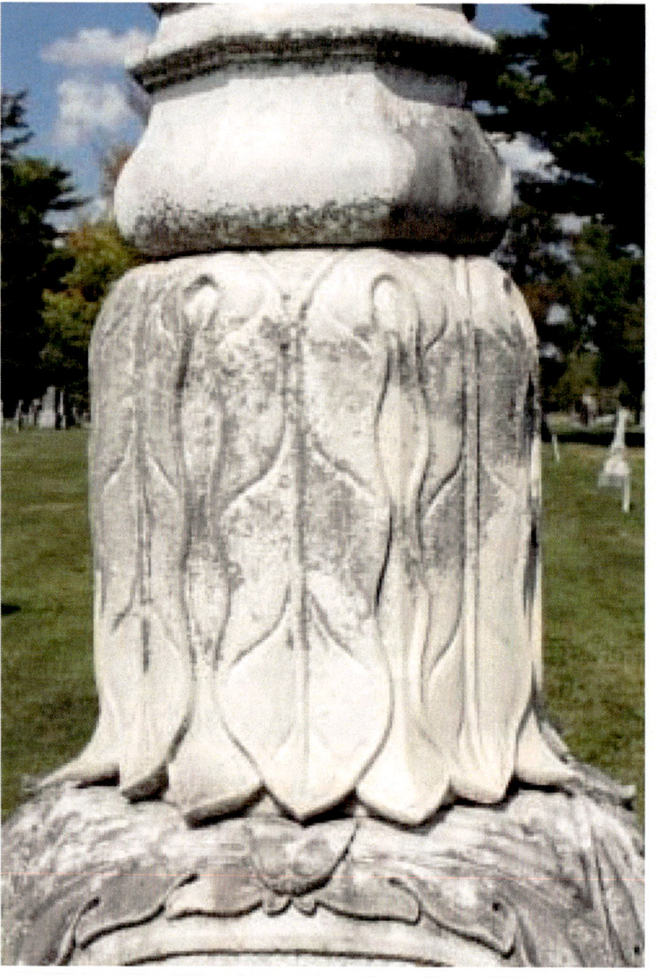

ACANTHUS LEAF

The *Acanthus mollis* is a common plant in the Mediterranean area, one of the oldest plants known in that area. The leaf of the acanthus is one of the most common plant forms to be used in stone carving and architectural decoration. Stylized acanthus leaf borders and scrolls are found extensively on grave markers in all section of the United States. Such design elements are to be found on friezes, dentils, and as capitals on columns.

Some of the popularity of the design is because the leaf was used so widely in classical Greek and Roman art. Probably the best known example is its architectural use on Corinthian and Composite capitals. However, the acanthus leaf also is one of the stylized carvings to be found, and many of the so-called "acanthus leaf" designs and symbols actually are quite imaginative. Often they are so altered as to be virtually unrecognizable. When an unrecognizable leaf design is found on a grave marker, chances are the carver or the monument dealer has labeled such a design as "acanthus leaf." Observers may disagree on whether a particular leaf design is acanthus or not, but there is a general acceptance of a variety of forms under the broad label.

In spite of this indefiniteness, the acanthus leaf is an appropriate symbol to use on grave markers. Because of the long life of the plant itself, it came to represent a long life for the person whose grave is so marked. In its original use, the acanthus leaf also meant long life and traditionally the plant was displayed at funeral ceremonies.

In Christian terms, the acanthus leaf came to be associated with sin because of the plant's thorns. It also is possible that on some occasions the acanthus leaf was used on a grave marker to indicate regeneration in another form, because acanthus roots send up additional growth since the plant is a perennial.

ANCHOR

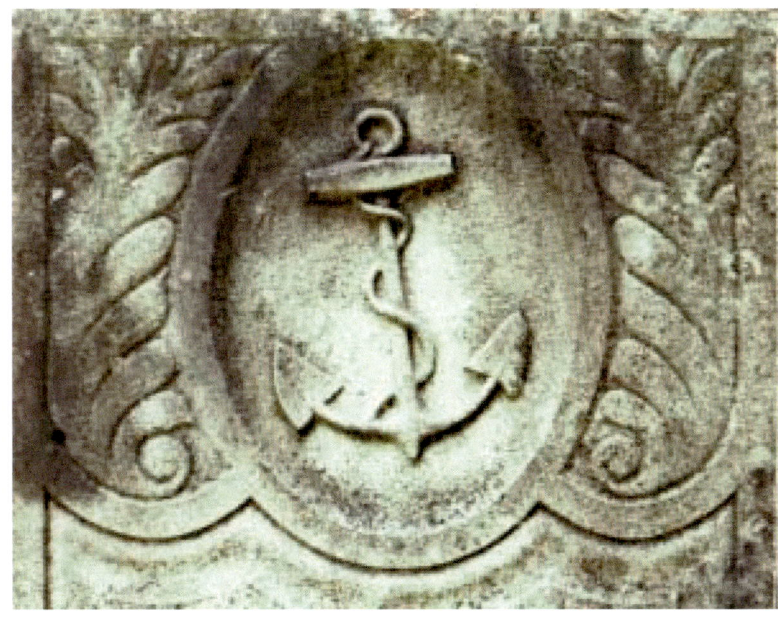

An anchor carved on a grave marker, unless accompanied by additional related symbols, rarely means that the deceased person buried in the grave had anything to do with the navy or the sea. Usually the anchor was used as a Christian symbol. An anchor was regarded in ancient times as a symbol of safety. Christians adopted the anchor as a symbol of hope, in this case the hope of salvation. In the common religious expression "Faith, Hope, and Charity," the anchor symbol is used for hope. The appropriate biblical reference is Hebrews 6:19, "We have this as a sure and steadfast anchor of the soul, a hope that enters into the inner place behind the curtain." St. Ambrose wrote: "As an anchor thrown from a ship prevents this from being borne about, but holds it securely, so faith, strengthened by hope..."

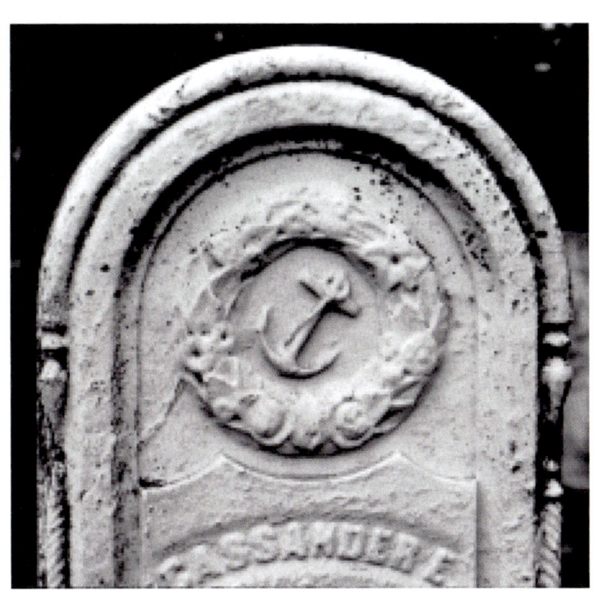

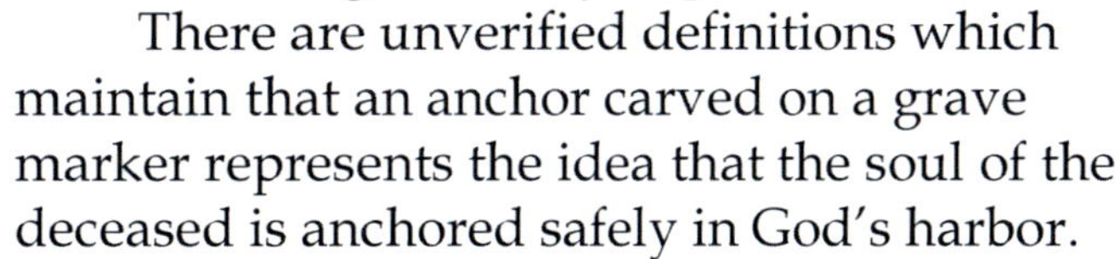

There are unverified definitions which maintain that an anchor carved on a grave marker represents the idea that the soul of the deceased is anchored safely in God's harbor.

Anchors of various designs frequently were carved on grave markers. Sometimes they seemed to be barely-concealed cross forms. The most frequently encountered anchor symbol design is one in which the upper extremity terminates in a ring adjoining the cross bar. The other end terminates in two curved branches with projectile points.

The anchor is one of several symbols also used by the Masonic order and other fraternal organizations. Sometimes the meaning in this context is to indicate the hope of a glorious immortality, after the storms of life have passed and the other shore has been reached.

ANGEL

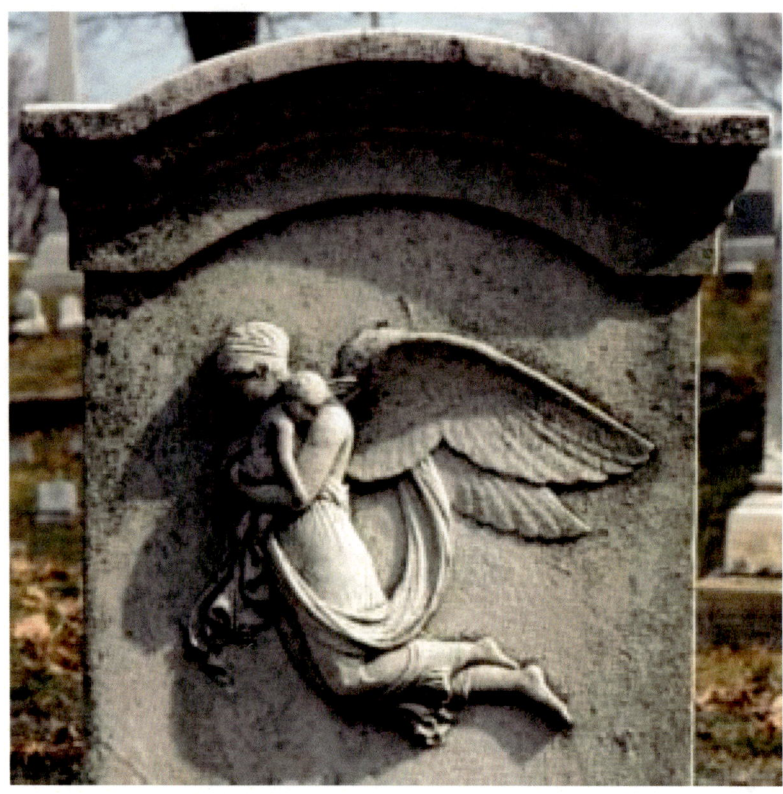

The symbol of an angel on a grave marker usually was intended to portray a messenger from God. An angel might be portrayed in ascending flight, in descending flight, or at repose over the grave site. Angels may be three-dimensional or depicted on the face of the memorial. Occasionally an angel was carved in relief on the face of a grave marker, symbolically carrying an effigy of the soul of the deceased person to Heaven. In such a case the effigy might bear a general resemblance to the deceased person as he or she appeared in life.

During the 18th and 19th centuries, it was believed that angels could be feminine, masculine, or neuter. Most of the statues and carvings show angels with wings. It is generally true that images of wings, such as on a dove, are a way of referring to messengers from God. (See "Dove," page 30)

A few statues and carvings show an angel holding a trumpet. (See "Trumpet," page 54)

Very rarely there are statues of angels writing in the Book of Life (See "Book of Life," page 22), representing the Recording Angel. In this case it was intended to demonstrate the record of good deeds done by the deceased person during his life.

Ordinarily angels on grave markers are shown wearing classical drapery. Very few are shown wearing clothing contemporary to the date of death on the marker.

There are a plethora of biblical references to angels, sometimes noted as an angel of the Lord, sometimes noted as an angel of God. Probably the most well-known reference is in Luke 2:9-11: "An angel of the Lord appeared to them, and the glory of the Lord shone around them, and they were terrified. But the angel said to them, 'Do not be afraid. I bring you good news that will cause great joy for all people. Today in the town of David a Savior has been born to you; he is the Messiah, the Lord.'" This famous story of the Nativity is vivid evidence of angels acting as messengers from God. Other significant biblical references include Matthew 13:39: "…the harvest is the end of the world; and the reapers are the angels," and Luke 16:22: "And it came to pass, that the beggar died, and was carried by the angels into Abraham's bosom; the rich man also died and was buried."

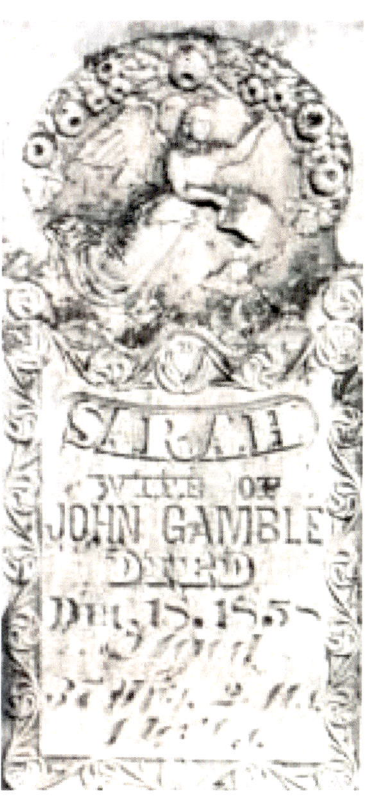

Additional biblical references to angels include Genesis 31:11, 22:11-16; Exodus 3:2, 14-19, 23:20; Numbers 20:16; Judges 2:1-2, 6:11; I Chronicles 21:15; Zechariah 1:12; Matthew 1:20; Luke 1:11-13, 16:22; and Revelation 1:1.

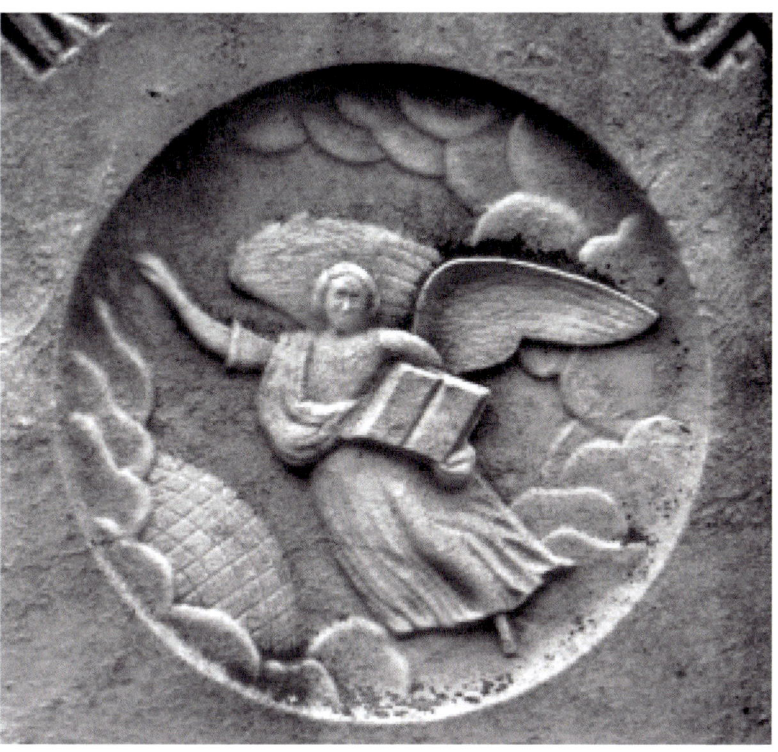

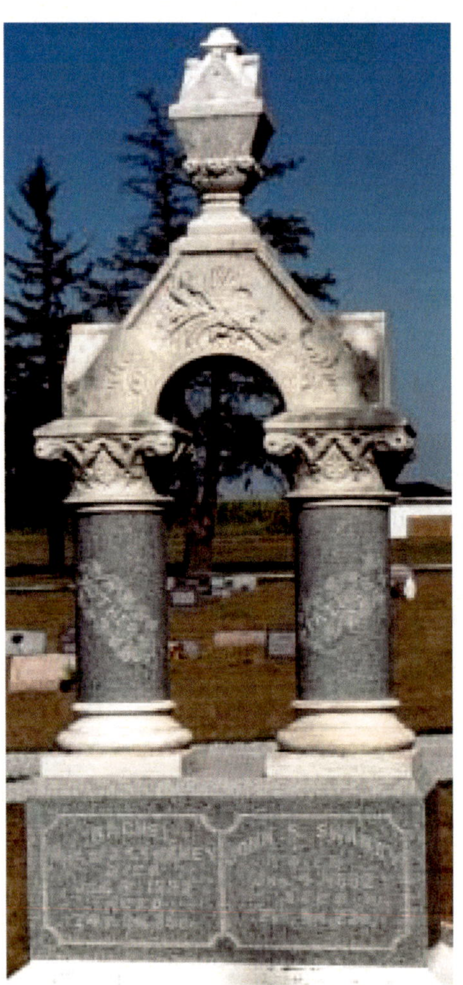

ARCH

The arch symbol most often is used to connect two columns or pillars. Throughout history the symbol of two columns has indicated a gateway to something significant, or a passageway to something sacred or holy or unusually important.

There are several interpretations of this type of grave marker. In the absence of other evidence, it usually indicates the eternal union of a wife and husband. The columns are found with smooth surfaces and also with fluted sides. Very occasionally columns are not round, but square. In either case there may be representations of ivy vines or garlands of flowers twining around the columns. In the case of a married couple, this is an additional symbol of their union through eternity.

Frequently the arch is shown with a pronounced keystone at its apex. Sometimes the keystone is surmounted by a symbolic urn. The urn is never a receptacle for cremains, but rather is a solid feature with symbolic significance. (See "Urn," page 56)

An arch with a keystone also is a significant symbol in the Masonic York Rite. When the Masonic arch connects two pillars, it refers to the building of the Temple of King Solomon. The two pillars represent Jachin and Boaz, and the arch, when secured by a keystone, is an emblem of completion. The biblical reference for the temple and the pillars is II Chronicles 3:15-17.

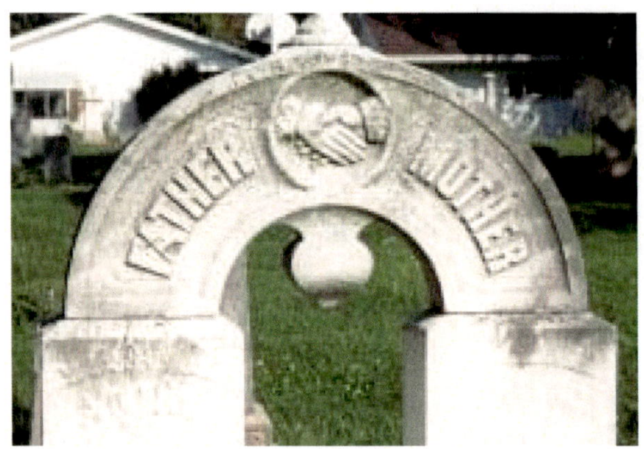

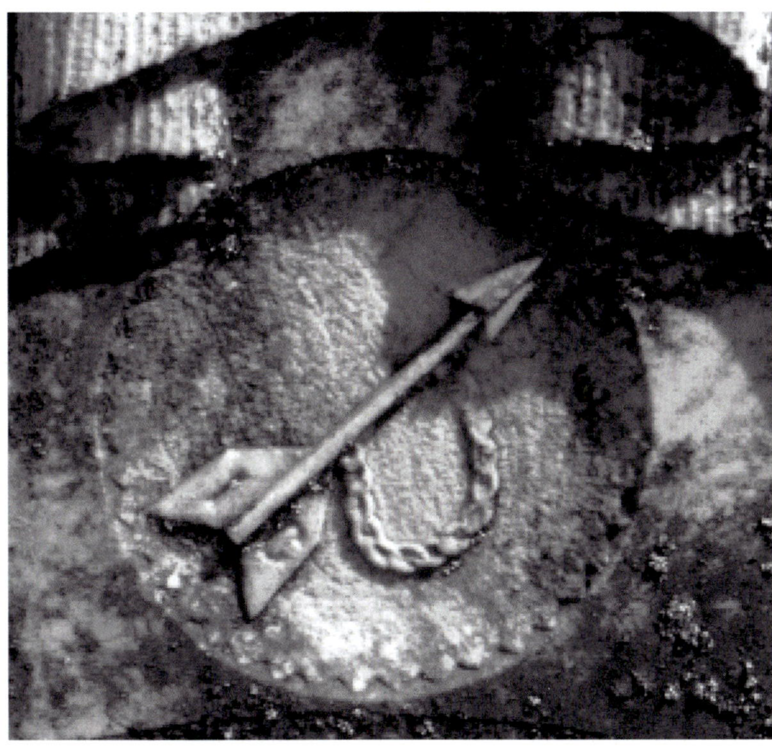

ARROW

When the symbol of an arrow is carved on a grave marker it usually does not have anything to do with the cause of the death of the person buried in the grave. It does, however, have mixed meanings, according to biblical references.

It may be the Christian symbol of the surety of the salvation of the soul of the deceased. II Kings 13:17: "And he said, the arrow of the Lord's deliverance. . . ." However, other biblical references point to the arrow as an instrument of God's judgment. Job 6:4: "The arrows of the Almighty are in me, my spirit drinks in their poison; God's terrors are marshaled against me." This interpretation is reinforced by Psalm 38:2, "Your arrows have pierced me, and your hand has come down on me."

Although the arrow is not a symbol commonly found on grave markers in Iowa or in the Midwest, there are instances of its use. It seems likely that the inspiration for those few examples come from a common familiarity with the Bible.

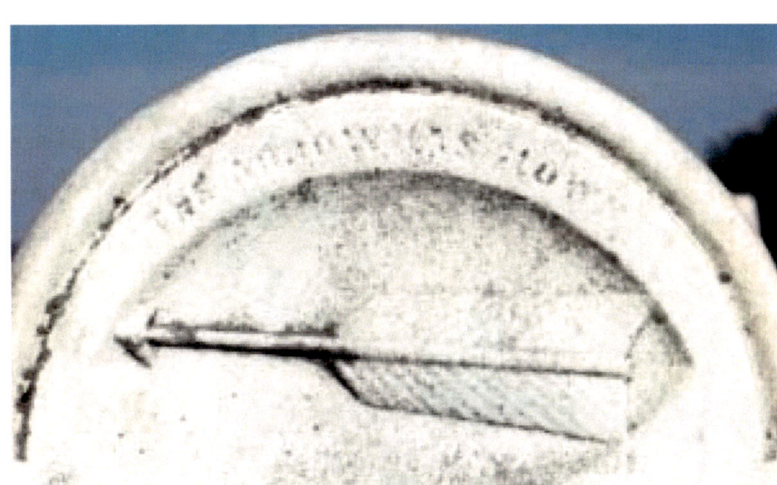

BOOK OF LIFE

Not all carved representations of books found on grave markers are intended to symbolize the Bible. If the words *Holy Bible* are carved on the pages of the book, then clearly that book is intended to represent the Bible. But if the words *Holy Bible* are not carved on the pages of the book, then perhaps the symbol was intended to represent the Book of Life. Such a book was the place where good deeds and bad deeds were recorded.

Since most Christian denominations tended to be optimistic about this sort of thing, the Book of Life commonly would be used to mark the graves of people whose good deeds obviously outnumbered their bad deeds or omissions. The Book of Life might be shown either in an open or a closed position.

Occasionally a treasured Bible verse, a portion from the text of the funeral sermon, or a favorite poem was carved on the open page. In folklore, it was believed that the number of pages of the Book of Life turned to the left helped to indicate the age of the deceased person. Since the biblical span of years was three score and ten, if the deceased was near the age of 70, then most of the pages would be turned over to the left. No doubt there were people who believed this to be true, but the majority of grave markers

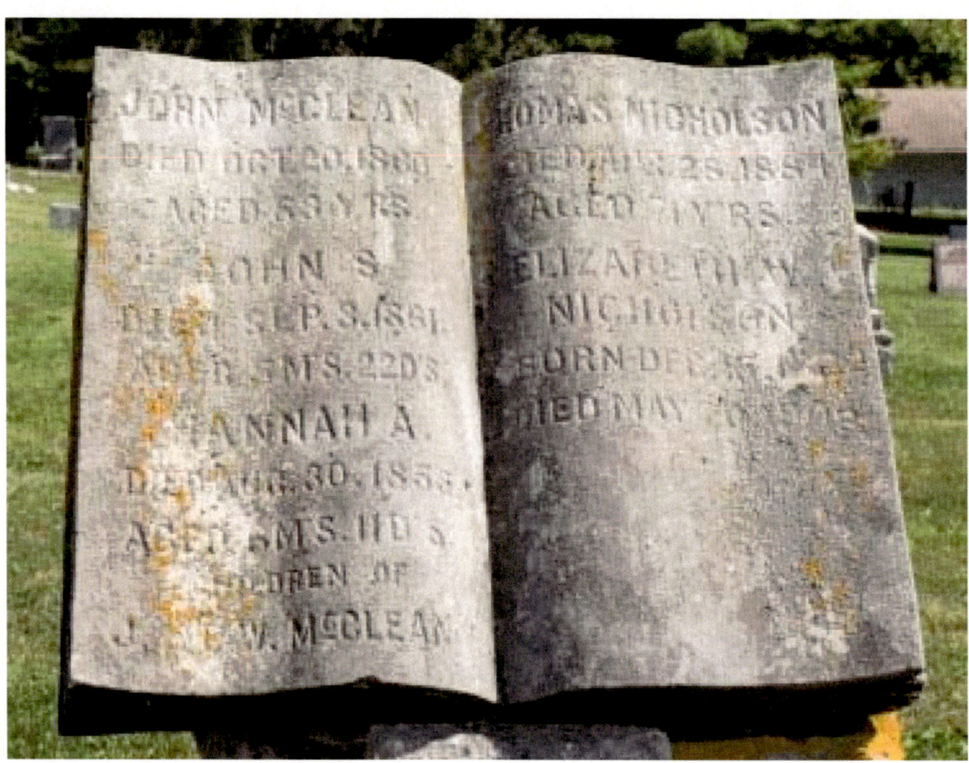

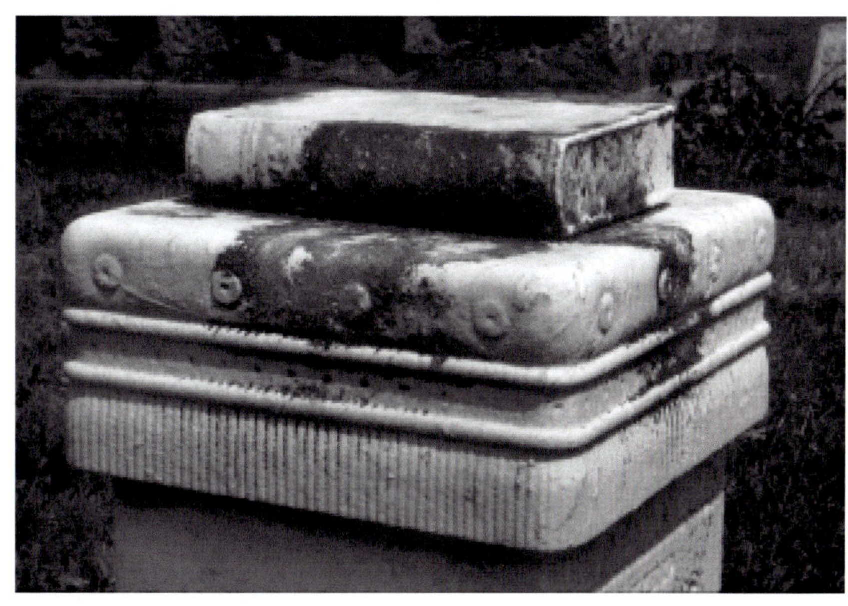

using the Book of Life symbol would not be included in this definition.

There are many biblical references to the Book of Life. Perhaps the most famous is Revelation 20:15: "Anyone whose name was not found written in the book of life was thrown into the lake of fire." Revelation 20:12:

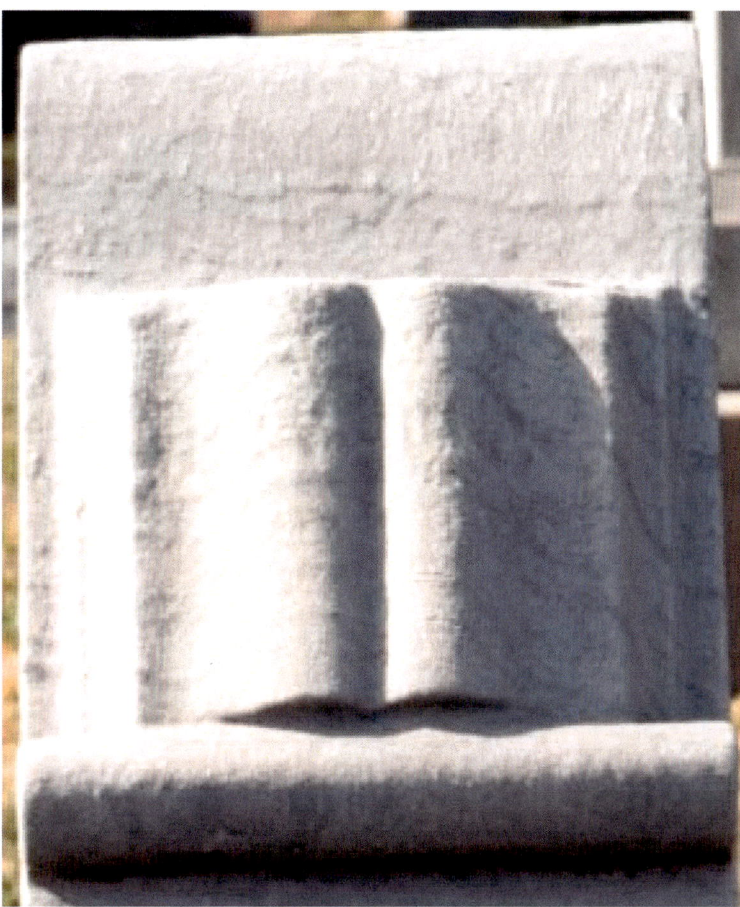

"And I saw the dead, great and small, standing before the throne, and books were opened, which is the book of life. The dead were judged according to what they had done as recorded in the books."

Other significant biblical references include: Exodus 32:32; Psalm 56:8, 69:27-28; Daniel 12:1; Ezekiel 9:2-6; Malachi 3:16-18; Philippians 4:3; Revelation 3:5; 17:8; 21:27, 22:19.

In the Masonic order, the open book symbolizes the revealed will of God. In this case the open book often rests on the bottom remnant of a broken column.

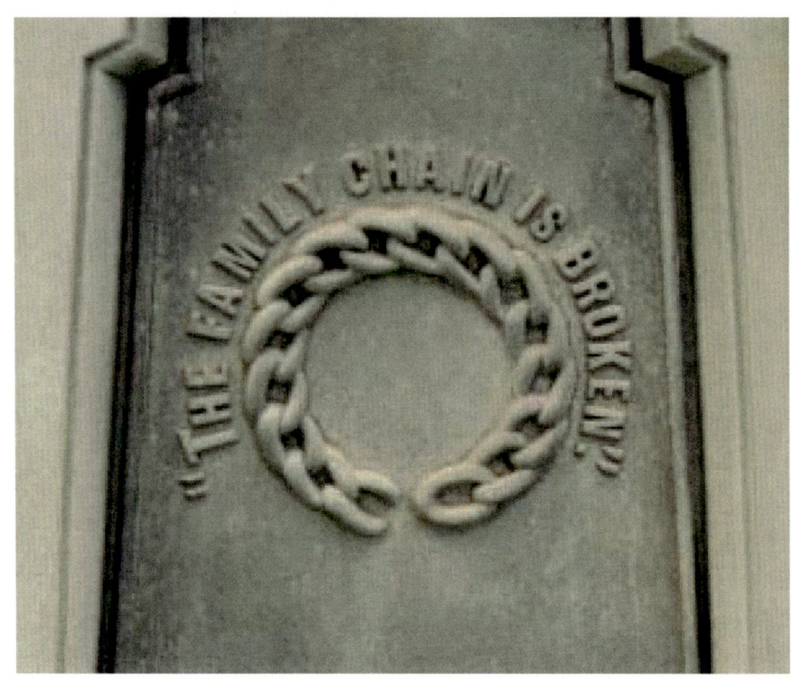

CHAIN

Two different styles of chain links appear as symbols on grave markers. When chain links carved on the face of a grave marker formed an intact circle, it meant that the nuclear family (wife, husband, and all of the children) were living. When a link was broken or removed it indicated that the family circle was no longer complete. The circle had been broken by the death of a family member. Sometimes the hand of God is portrayed reaching down from heaven to pluck a link from the family circle.

At times, chains were carved on an otherwise undecorated grave marker, and in that case the chains were simply used for decoration.

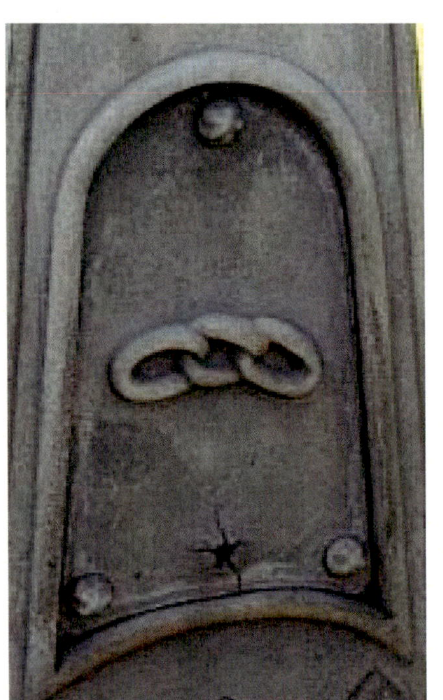

The circular chain in completed form should never be confused with the common symbol of three chain links in an arc, which was a symbol of the Independent Order of Odd Fellows (IOOF), a fraternal lodge. Often the letters F, L, and T were carved within the chain links of an IOOF marker. These letters stand for friendship, love, and truth. In that case the symbol represents the major purpose and principle of the lodge. There are occasions when this arc of three links is found on a grave marker that also portrays the Masonic symbol of the compass and square. Apparently some men belonged to both organizations. There is also fragmentary evidence that the three-link arc may have been a symbol of the Masonic order.

Many of the IOOF chain arcs turn downward. A few examples have been located which show the chain arc turned upward, and a very few where the chain links form a straight line.

CLOCK

A clock face carved on a grave marker is one of the several indications of the passing of time. Others include hour glasses with or without wings, sun dials, calendars, and other means of measuring time. All measurers of time had the same general intent, to emphasize the mortality of humans. Time passed, and time was running out for this life.

During the 19th century, folklore held that when a death occurred in a house the clocks stopped. Since a majority of deaths during that century did occur in the home, this became a widely-entrenched belief. In a sense time had stopped for the person who had died. The belief was further elaborated to mean that if the clock did not stop of its own accord, then it should be manually stopped at the moment of death. No clock in the household was to be started again until after the burial of the person who had died. At that point, the clock had to be manually started at a time different from the time of the death. If these procedures were not followed, so the belief continued, another person in that same household – the person manually starting the clock at the same moment as the death – would die before another twelve months had elapsed.

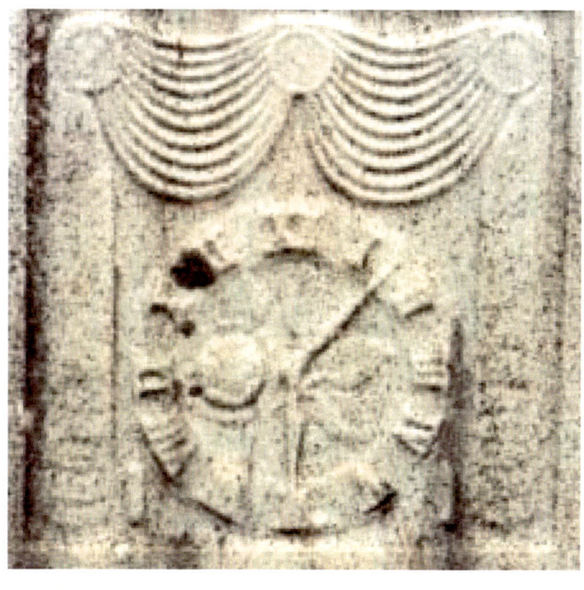

One famous manifestation of this belief is in the song *My Grandfather's Clock:* It stopped short, never to go again, when the old man died.

A curious alternative to stopping the clock was to turn the clock face to the wall for the prescribed period of time.

A custom similar to the stopped clock was the Victorian practice of either turning all of the mirrors in the house with face to the wall or draping them with black cloths. The mirrors were to remain so until after the burial of the deceased. All windows facing public roadways also had to be draped in black.

Although most people in the 21st century do not believe this sort of folklore, a number of people still continue these customs. Perhaps the idea is that it is better to be safe than sorry.

There were many more folklore customs and beliefs connected with death which continued to be perpetuated in the dozens of etiquette books and almanacs printed during the latter half of the 19th century.

COLUMN

Columns or pillars (the words may be used interchangeably) are architectural elements which have been adapted to serving as grave markers. (See "Arch," page 20) When a column appears singly and is complete with a capital at the top, the person whose grave it marks has reached the biblically-expected span of years, three score and ten. In that sense this particular life span is complete.

When the column is incomplete or is carved to appear broken, the most common interpretation is that the person whose grave it marks died prematurely, before she/he reached the age of 70 years.

There are unverified explanations that claim when a column is broken and both sections are represented, the age of the deceased may be reckoned. The column section still standing supposedly shows the age at death, while the toppled section of the column shows the years up to 70 that had not yet been lived. This interpretation is not generally accepted by scholars of grave marker art.

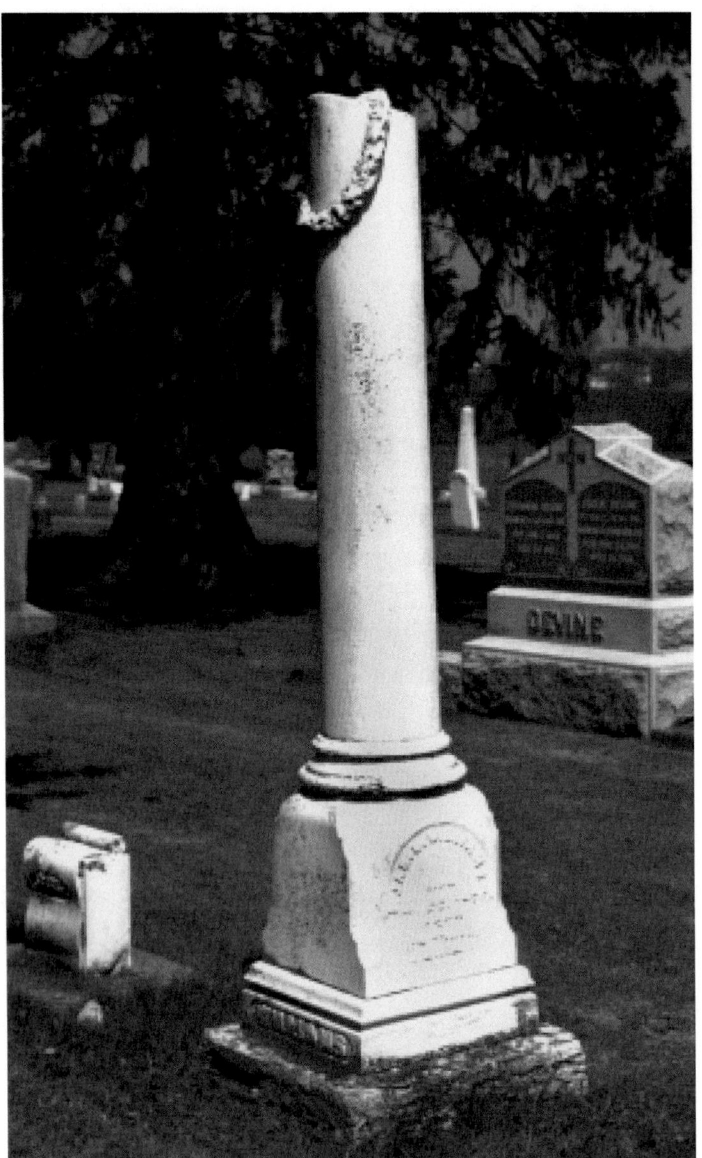

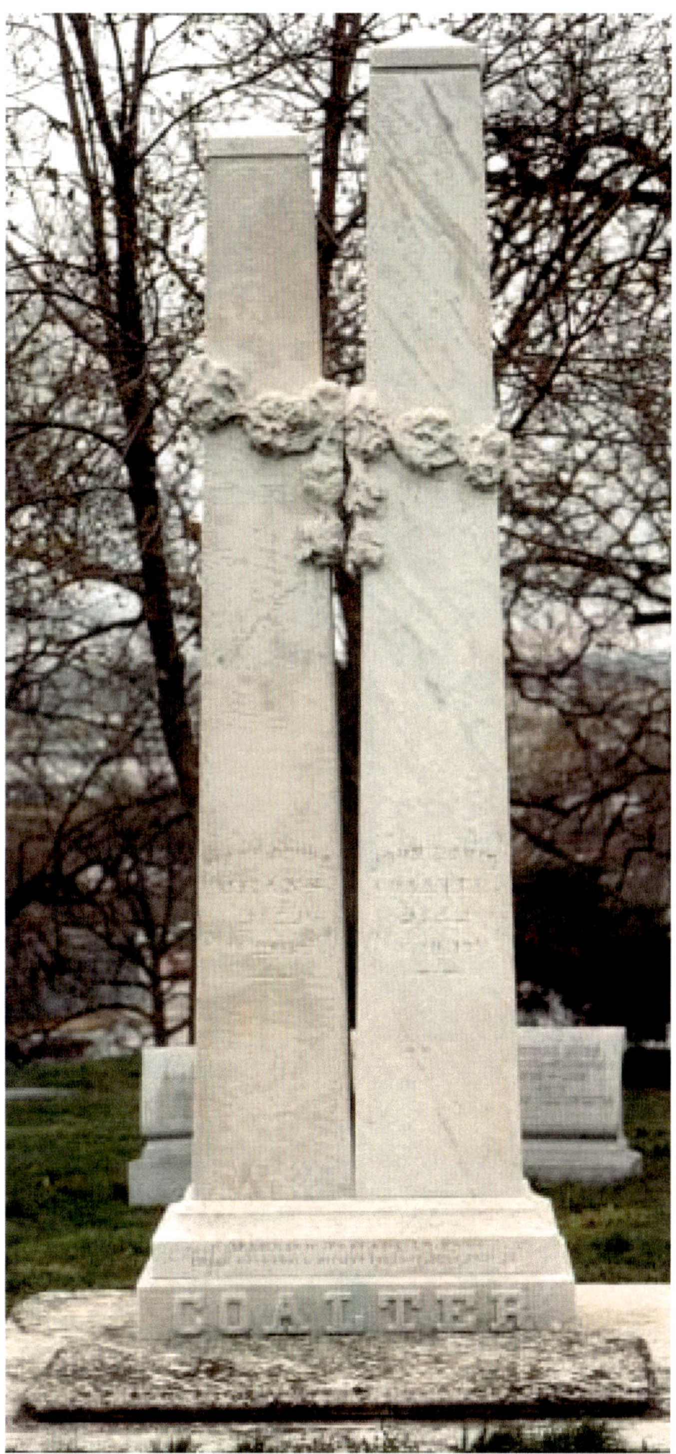

Yet another interpretation of a column or pillar is that it marks the passage between life and death, the transition from this world to another world. In Christianity this means the passage from earth to heaven. In this way the column is quite similar to the drapery or stage curtain, and the gate. These designs also commonly are interpreted to mark the passage from life as we know it and the afterlife.

There are many biblical passages which refer to columns or pillars, but most of them are about actual buildings, particularly temples. Genesis 35:14 is about Jacob setting up a stone pillar in the place where God had spoken to him. Revelation 3:12 infers that a person who is "saved" becomes a pillar in the temple of God.

Classical architecture of Greece and Rome is rife with columns. Some examples are attempts to reach closer to heaven, and therefore valuable or honored people or objects were placed at the top. In Rome especially, the statues of heroes often are placed on top of pillars for greater honor. When a grave marker consists of paired columns there is another whole dimension of meaning. (See "Arch," page 20)

CROWN

In the symbolism of the 19th century, a crown represented the victory of eternal life over death. Various designs of crowns appear on grave markers; the most common being the medieval circlet. That may have been a practical matter rather than an artistic choice. Medieval circlet crowns were easier to carve than those which resemble St. Edward's crown, used in the coronation of English monarchs.

When a crown is shown with a cross through it, the symbol probably represents membership in the Knights Templar.

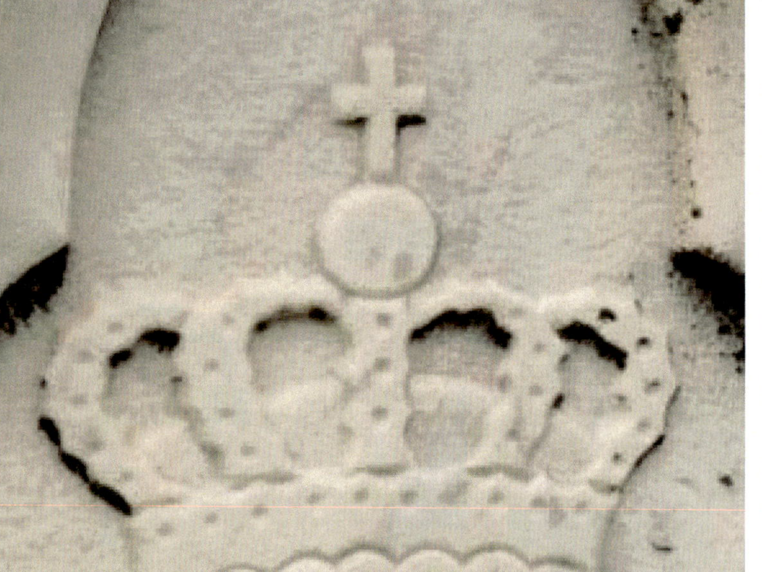

Almost all crowns on grave markers are carved in relief rather than three-dimensional. It is rare for a crown motif to be incised into the surface of the stone. The crown symbol is quite common on grave markers cast in white bronze.

A vast number of biblical references mention crowns. There are at least eight different sorts of crowns portrayed in these passages. For instance, there are crowns of glory, of victory, of life, of splendor, of righteousness, and of joy. Also there are crowns of loving kindness and tender mercies, and crowns which last forever. Among the better known biblical references to crowns is I Peter 5:4: "And when the Chief Shepherd appears, you will receive the crown of glory that will never fade away." Another notable verse is Revelation 2:10: "Be thou faithful unto death, and I will give thee a crown of life." Yet another example is II Timothy 4:8: "Henceforth there is laid up for me a crown of righteousness, which the Lord, the righteous judge, shall give me at that day."

Other biblical references to crowns include Psalm 103:4, 149:4; Proverbs 4:7-9;

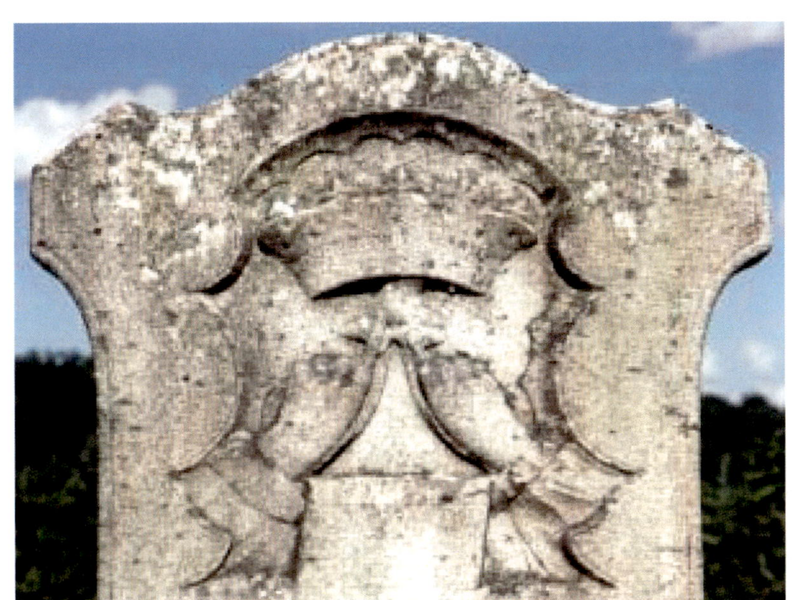

Isaiah 28:5, 62:3; I Corinthians 9:24-25; I Thessalonians 2:19-20; James 1:12; I Peter 5:4; and Revelation 2:10. It is apparent from these few examples that crowns were thought to be important to Christians throughout history. That may be especially true of the 19th century. Christian thought, particularly Protestant Christian thought, would have been eager to draw upon these biblical references when choosing symbols to place on grave markers of that time.

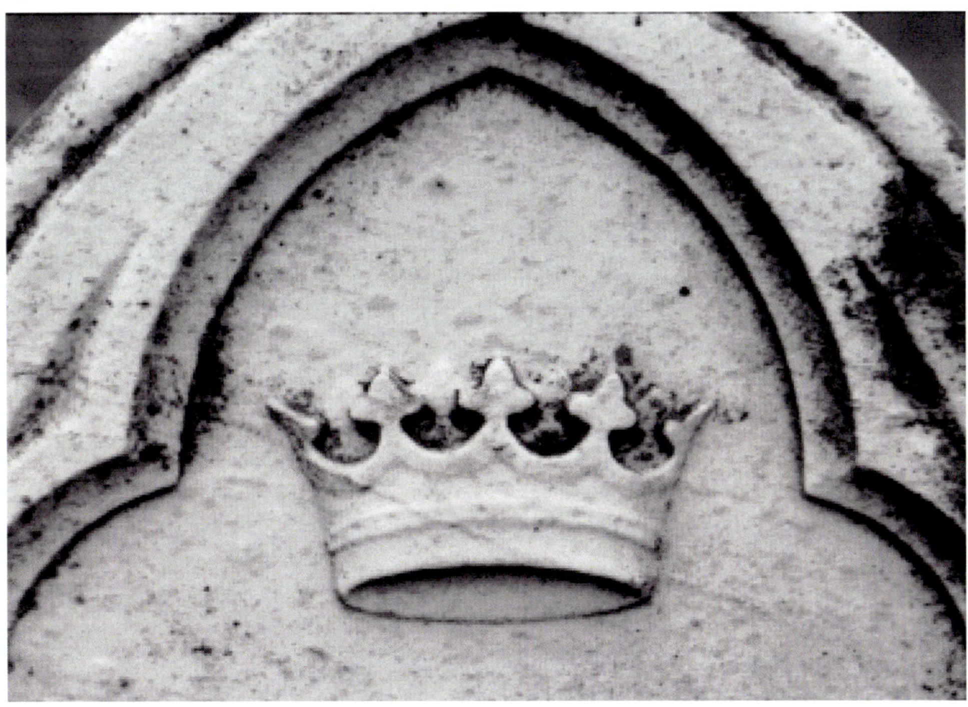

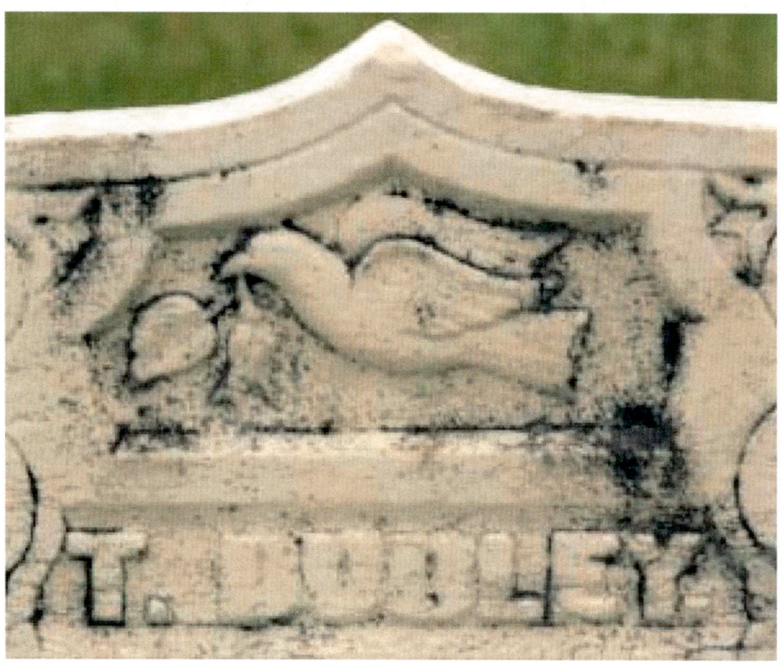

DOVE

In ancient and classical periods of history, a dove often was known as a symbol of peace. This same definition continued into the Christian era. However, during the last two thousand years, the dove as a symbol has come to have additional meanings. When interpreting 19th century grave markers, it should be assumed that the dove represented the Holy Spirit, but sometimes it also meant that the dove was a messenger from God. Winged symbols often were used at that time to mean messengers from God, with other layers of meaning contributing to this definition.

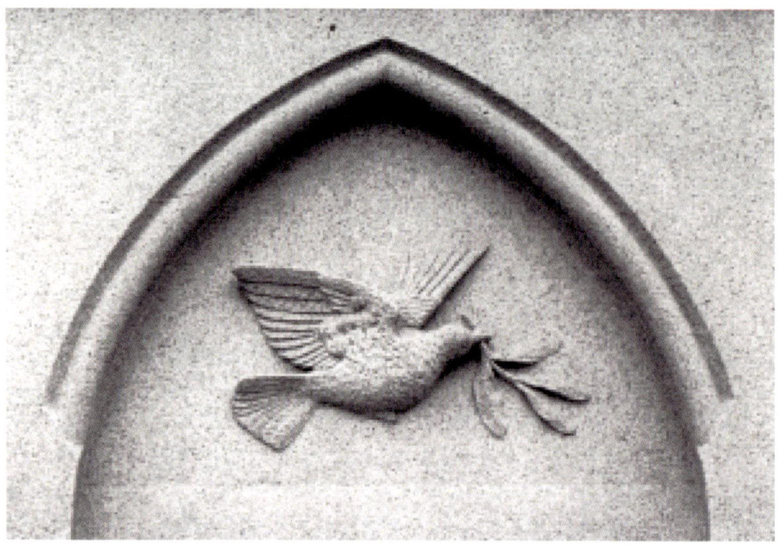

But of course a dove continued to act as a symbol of peace. On grave markers doves were portrayed as ascending, descending, or at rest. There are examples of doves being carved as dead. Doves might carry olive branches in their beaks, or they might be shown carrying a riband in their beak with the words "Rest in Peace" on the folds. Among the most poignant symbols involving

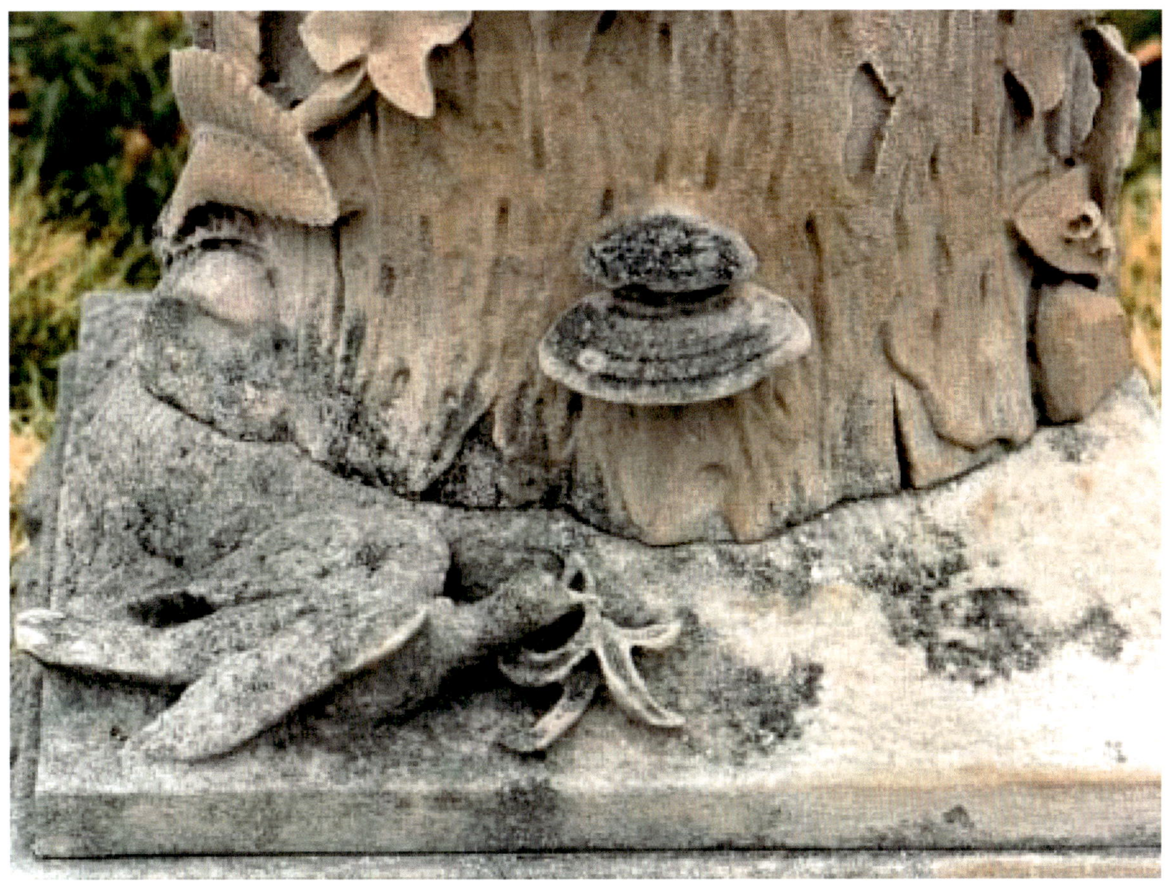

doves are those which represent the dove carrying a rose bud in its beak. This meant the death of a baby or a very young child.

Biblical references to doves abound. Matthew 3:16: "And, lo, the heavens were opened unto him and he saw the spirit of God descending like a dove, and lighting on him." Mark 1:10: "He saw the heavens opened, and the spirit like a dove descending upon him." Luke 3:22: "And, the Holy Ghost descended in a bodily shape like a dove upon him." John 1:32: "I saw the spirit descending from heaven like a dove and it abode upon him." Additional biblical references to doves include Genesis 8:11 and Psalm 68:13. The latter verse is one of the more colorful references. "Even while you sleep among the sheep pens, the wings of my dove are sheathed with silver, its feathers with shining gold."

GATES

Gates, like doors, are an indication of passage from one place to another place. When used as a symbol on grave markers, gates invariably are shown as being open. This was intended to mark the passage between life as we know it and eternal life. Sometimes the scene beyond the gate is shown as the heavenly city, or a profile of it. That the gates lead to heaven is indicated by the presence of the sun, the moon, a star, or a crown. All of these objects are indications of the triumph of eternal life over death. Each has a specific meaning (See "Sun," page 50, "Moon," page 43, "Star," page 49, and "Crown," page 28)

Sometimes gates are shown with steps beyond, what is referred to in some Christian hymns as the "golden stairs." Gates were shown with elaborate gate posts and arches, representing the gates of heaven, colloquially referred to as the "pearly gates." When the soul of the deceased passed through the gate, it passed from earthly life to life eternal. Revelation 21:2: "And I John saw the Holy City, New Jerusalem, coming down from God out of Heaven."

Sometimes it is difficult to differentiate between gates and stairways because they often occur together. Biblical references to gates are numerous. Psalm 24:7: "Lift up your heads, O ye gates, and be ye lift up, ye everlasting doors; and the King of glory shall come in." Psalm 118:19: "Open for the gates of the righteous; I will enter and give thanks to the Lord." Psalm 118:20: "This is the gate of the Lord, into which the

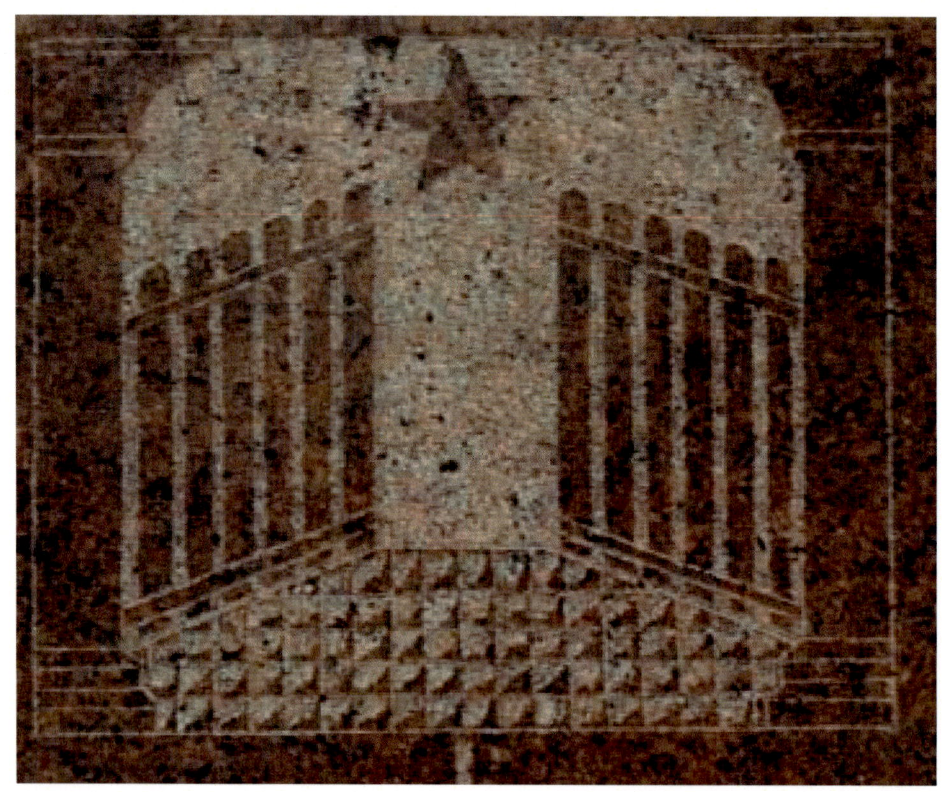

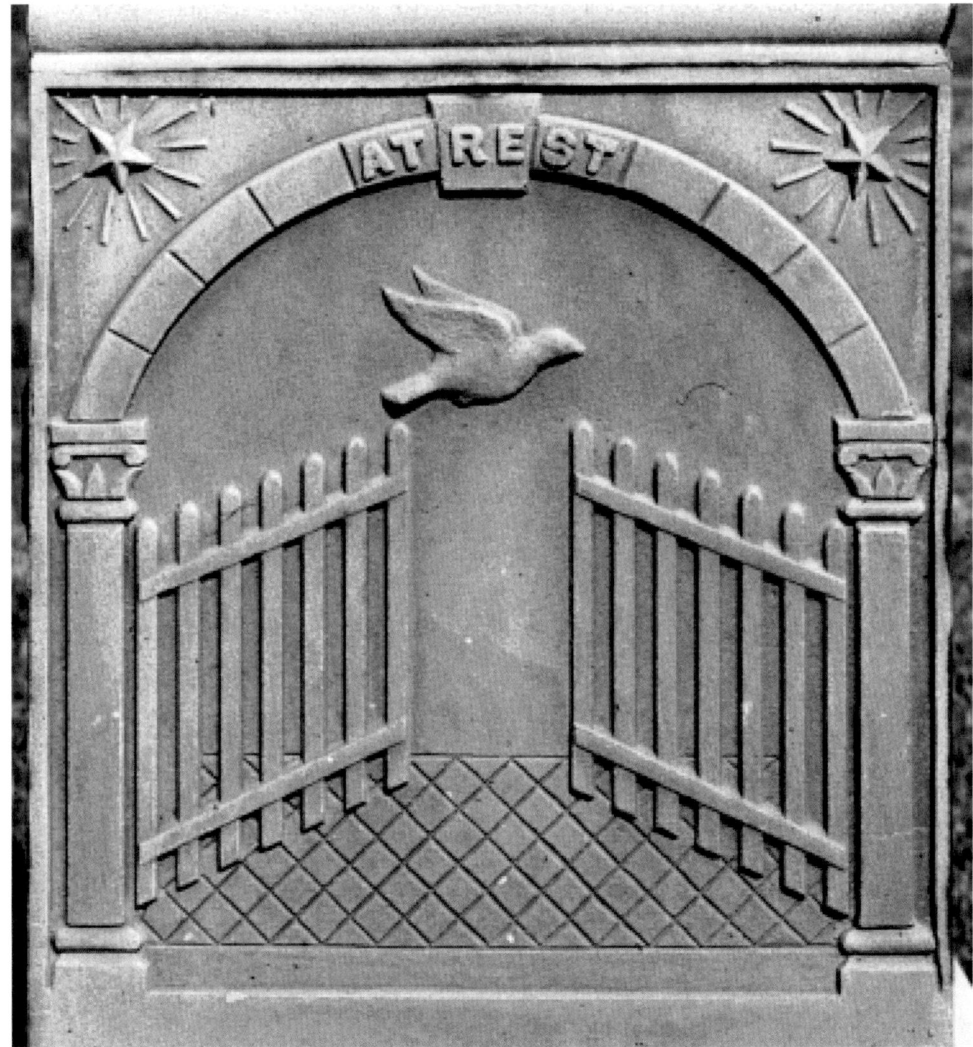

righteous shall enter."

Additional references include Isaiah 26:2: "Open the gates that the righteous nation may enter, the nation that keeps faith," and Jeremiah 7:2, "Stand in the gate of the Lord's house, and proclaim there this word, and say, "Hear the word of the Lord, all ye of Judah, that enter in at these gates to worship the Lord."

There also are New Testament references to gates. John 10:9: "I am the gate; whoever enters through me will be saved," Revelation 21:25: "And the gates of it shall not be shut at all by day; for there shall be no night there," and Revelation 22:14: "Blessed are they that do His commandments, that they may have right to the tree of life, and may enter in through the gates into the city."

The most famous biblical example of a stairway is Genesis 28:12, when Jacob "…had a dream in which he saw a stairway resting on the earth, with its top reaching to heaven, and the angels of God were ascending and descending on it."

It is safe to conclude that any symbol on a grave marker which represents a passage of any sort is intended to mark the passage from life, through death, to eternal life. Since the majority of Christians in the 19th century seem to have been optimistic and positive in outlook, all of these passages showed a belief that the soul of the deceased had passed into heaven.

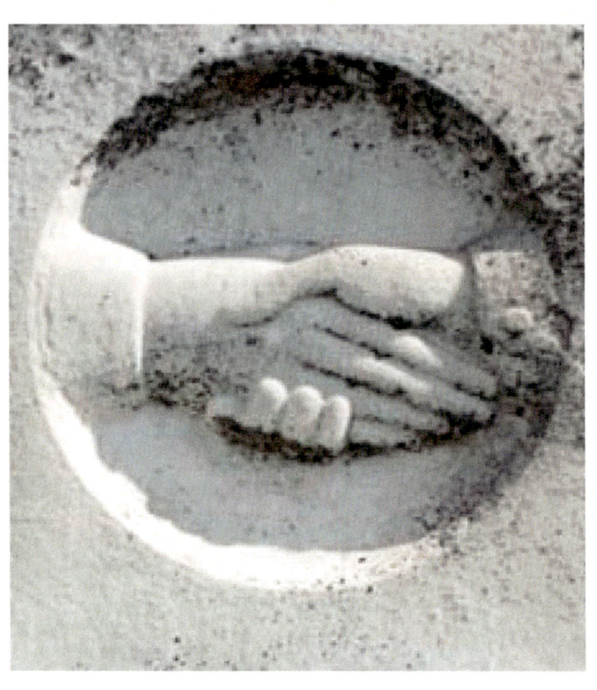

HANDS

There are many alternative meanings for hands as a symbol on a grave marker. It depends upon the positions of the hands and the fingers, and whether or not the hand is holding an object.

If the hand is shown with the index finger pointing upward, it was intended to give assurance that the soul of the person buried in the grave was safe in heaven. If the index finger or the entire hand is portrayed as reaching down, it is the representation of God's hand reaching down to lift the soul of the deceased to heaven. Sometimes God's hand is portrayed as reaching down and plucking a link of chain from the family circle. (see "Chain," page 24)

Often two hands are shown clasped together. This symbol has been interpreted in several plausible ways. It may mean the union of a wife and husband through eternity. It may mean the clasp of friendship, because of membership in the same lodge. It may mean the blessing of the church on the soul of the deceased. It is necessary to examine the cuffs on the clasped hands to help understand which meaning was intended.

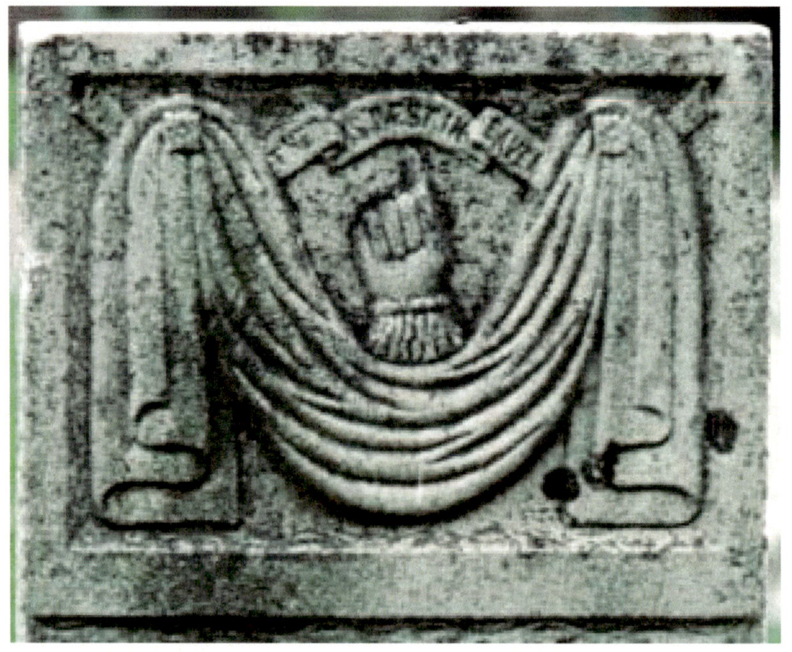

If a large hand with an elaborate or ornate cuff is enclosing a smaller hand with a plainer cuff, it is likely to symbolize the church, blessing the soul of the person buried in that grave. It also may mean the farewell of a parent to a

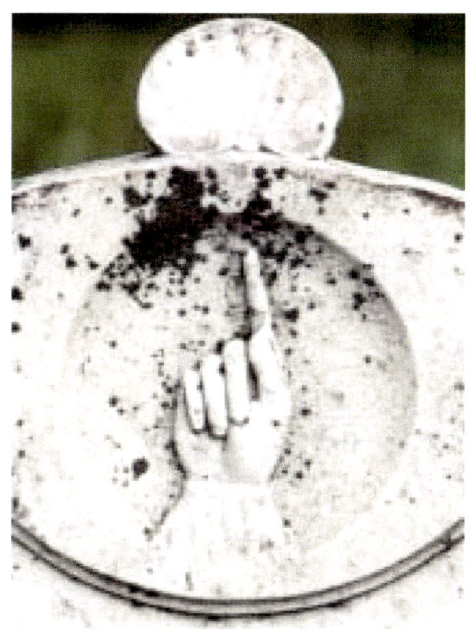

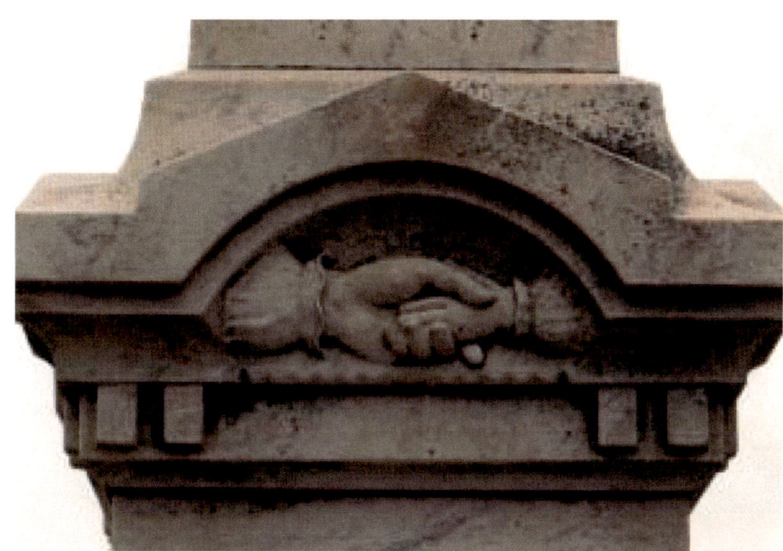

deceased child. If one cuff is ornamented in a feminine style, then it is most likely it is the symbol of the union of a married couple.

There are a great many variations of these basic interpretations of the clasped hands symbol. And there is always the possibility that this symbol was chosen solely because the person ordering the carving simply liked the image.

Hands also may be shown on grave markers holding a variety of objects. The most common examples are a hand holding a flower, an open book, or a torch. There are rare examples of a hand holding a quill pen. Whatever the object in the hand is, the importance is likely to be centered on the object, not on the hand. In more recent years there are a few examples of hands on a grave marker holding tools. Probably the intended meaning is to focus on an occupation related to the particular tool.

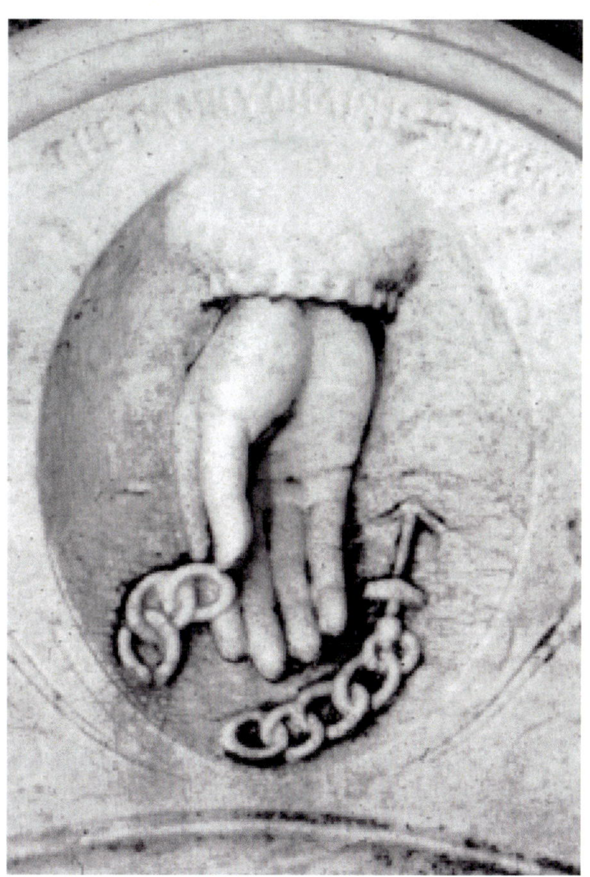

HARP

Portrayal of musical instruments was not common on grave markers. There was the occasional trumpet (see "Trumpet," page 54), and the even more occasional harp. The harp was not a common musical instrument in the 19th century home. But the Bible has many references to harps, the symbol of joy and celebration. Of course this joy was not because of the death, but rather the confidence that the soul was safe in heaven. The harp is also a symbol of praise to God.

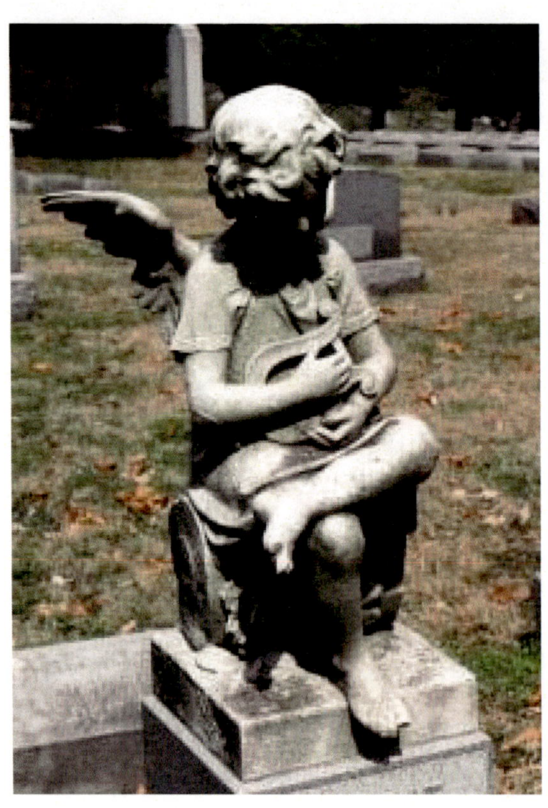

Biblical references to harps are so numerous that a few examples will suffice to explain and support the symbol's meaning. I Chronicles 13:8: "David and all the Israelites were celebrating with all their might before God, with songs and with harps, lyres, timbrels, cymbals, and trumpets." I Chronicles 15:16: "David told the leaders of the Levites to appoint their fellow Levites as musicians to make a joyful sound with musical instruments; lyres, harps, and cymbals." Psalm 33:2: "Praise the Lord with harp: sing unto him with the psaltery and an instrument of ten strings." Psalm 43:4: "Then will I go unto the altar of God, unto God my exceeding joy: yea, upon the harp will I praise thee, O God my God." Psalm 71:22: "I will praise you with the harp for your faithfulness, my God; I will sing praise to you with the lyre, Holy One of Israel." Psalm 81:2: "Begin the music, strike the timbrel, play the melodious harp and lyre." Psalm 92:1-4: "It is good to praise the Lord and make music to your name, O Most High, proclaiming your love in the morning and your faithfulness at night, to the music of the ten-stringed lyre and the melody of the harp. For you make me glad by your deed, Lord; I sing for joy at what your hands have done." Psalm 108:1-2: "My heart, O God, is steadfast; I will sing and make music with all my soul. Awake, harp and lyre! I will awaken the dawn." Psalm 144:9, "I will sing a new song to You, O God; On a harp of ten strings I will sing praises to You." Perhaps the most famous biblical reference to harps is found in Psalm 150:3-5: "Praise him with the sounding of the trumpet, praise him with the harp and lyre, praise

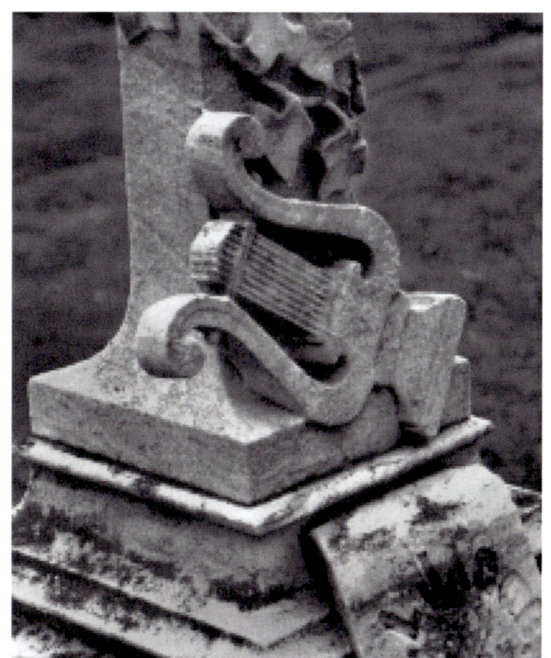

him with timbrel and dancing, praise him with the strings and pipe, praise him with the clash of cymbals, praise him with resounding cymbals."

All of these references are to be found in the Old Testament. The New Testament contains one significant passage about the harp. Revelation 14:2: ". . . and I heard a voice from Heaven, as the voice of many waters, and as the voice of a great thunder; and I heard the voice of harpers harping on their harps."

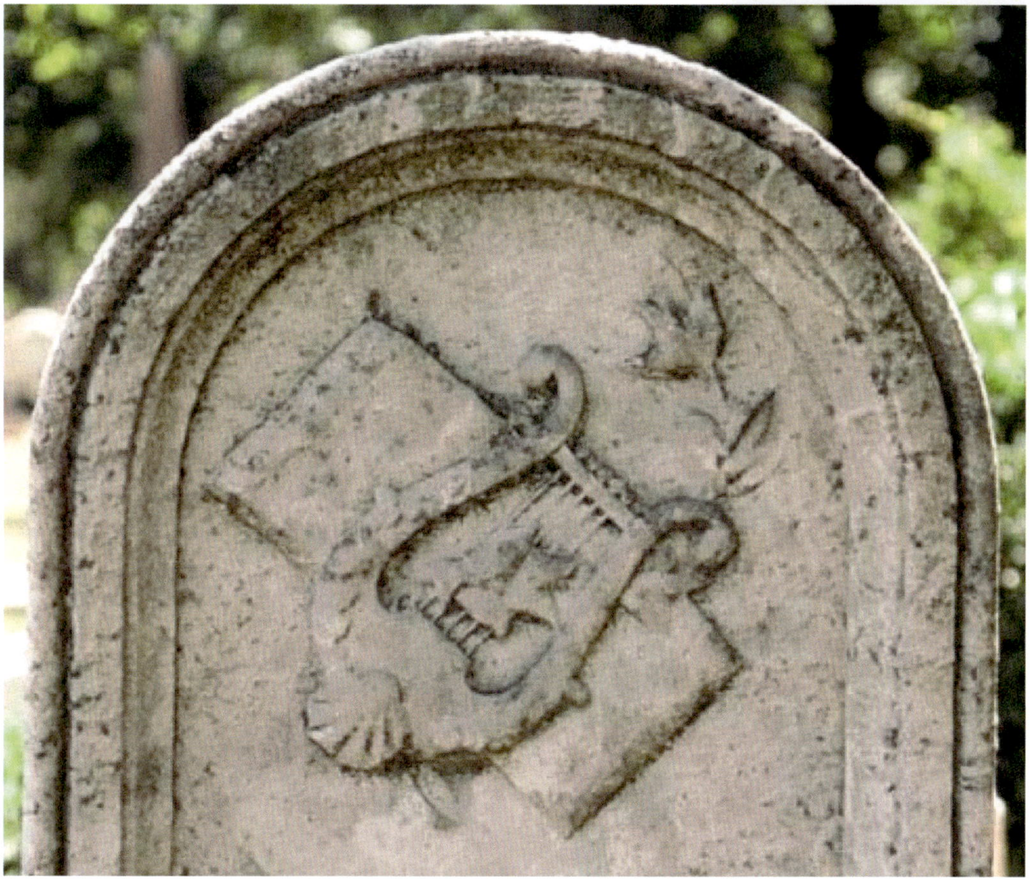

HEAVENLY CITY

Many grave markers, particularly after 1890, show the outline or skyline of the heavenly city, e.g. heaven. Many of these representations are in the background, with a gateway, gate, and/ or stairs leading up towards the city in the distance. Also portrayed may be a star, a moon, or a crown, representing God's presence in heaven. (See "Gates," page 32, "Star," page 49, "Moon," page 43, "Crown," page 28)

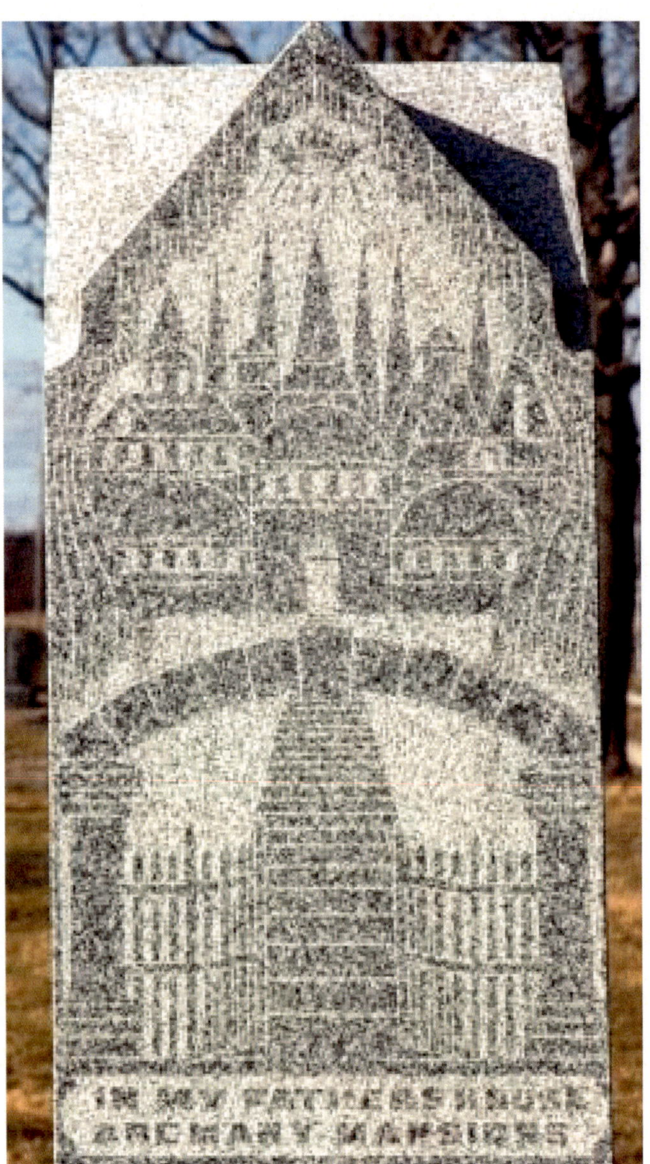

This symbol was intended to demonstrate the assurance that the soul of the deceased person had gone to heaven.

Revelation 21:2 presents a scene of the heavenly city: "I saw the Holy City, the new Jerusalem, coming down out of heaven from God, prepared as a bride beautifully dressed for her husband."

Outlines of the heavenly city on grave markers are remarkably similar. They represent what people in the latter half of the 19th century envisioned the appearance of heaven. Most of these scenes are rather lightly etched in granite. Sometimes they are so lightly etched that it is hard to see them clearly.

This symbol began to appear on grave markers only after technology made it possible to etch images in granite surfaces.

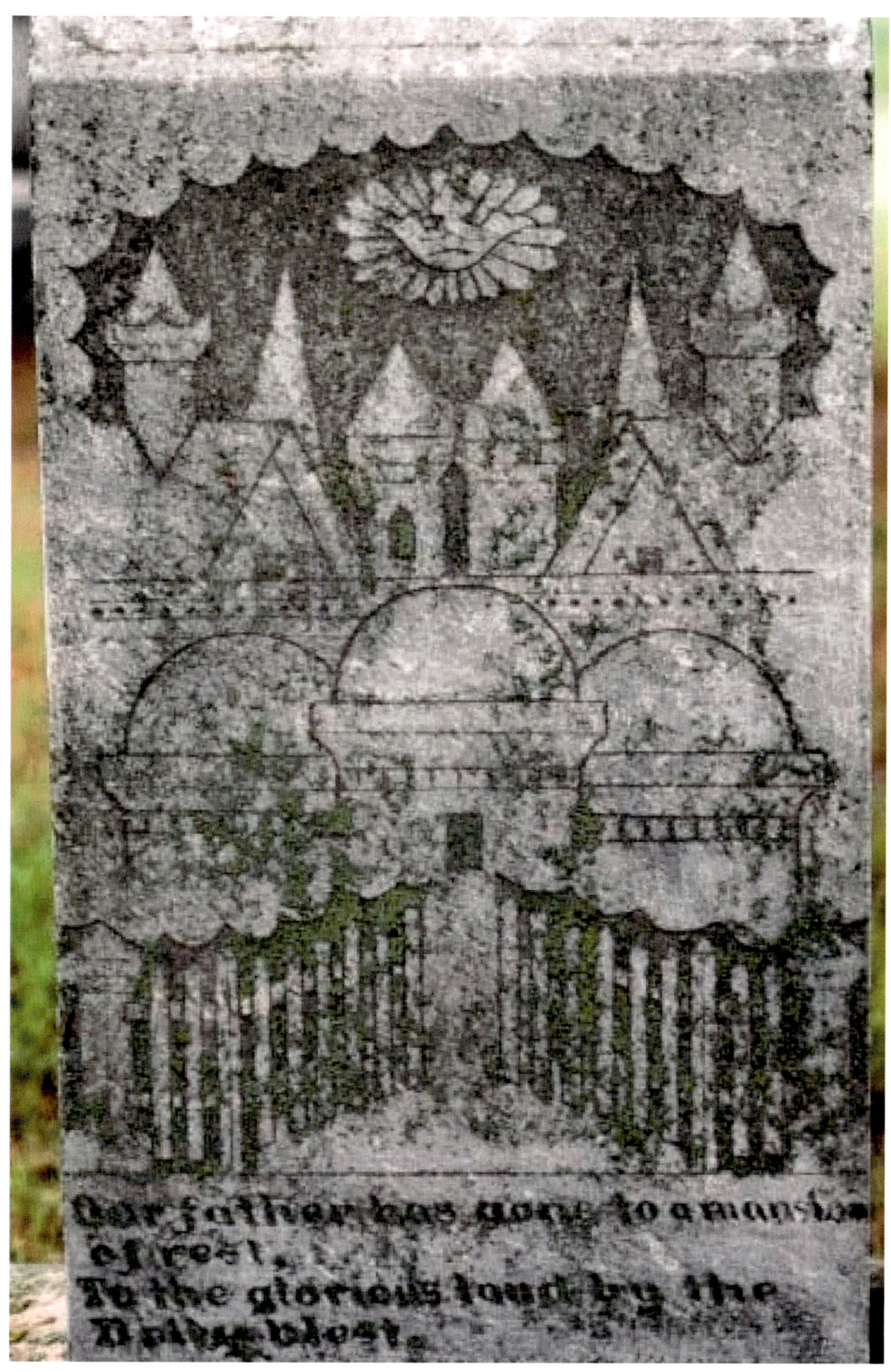
Our father has gone to a
of rest.
To the glorious land by the
blest.

LAMB

A lamb on a grave marker quite often marks the burial place of a baby or a very young child. The use of this symbol for the graves of babies was common throughout the 19th, 20th, and 21st centuries. Since a lamb is the symbol of innocence, the inference is that because of their young age the baby was innocent of sin.

Lambs also are used to indicate sacrifice, but this meaning seems to be much less frequent that the correlation with innocence. There also seem to be instances of the use of the lamb on a grave marker for an adult who perhaps was mentally challenged and the family felt that he/she had the mind of a child.

It is almost impossible to discuss the symbolic meaning of the lamb without including a discussion of shepherds and sheep. Where the lamb is used as a symbol

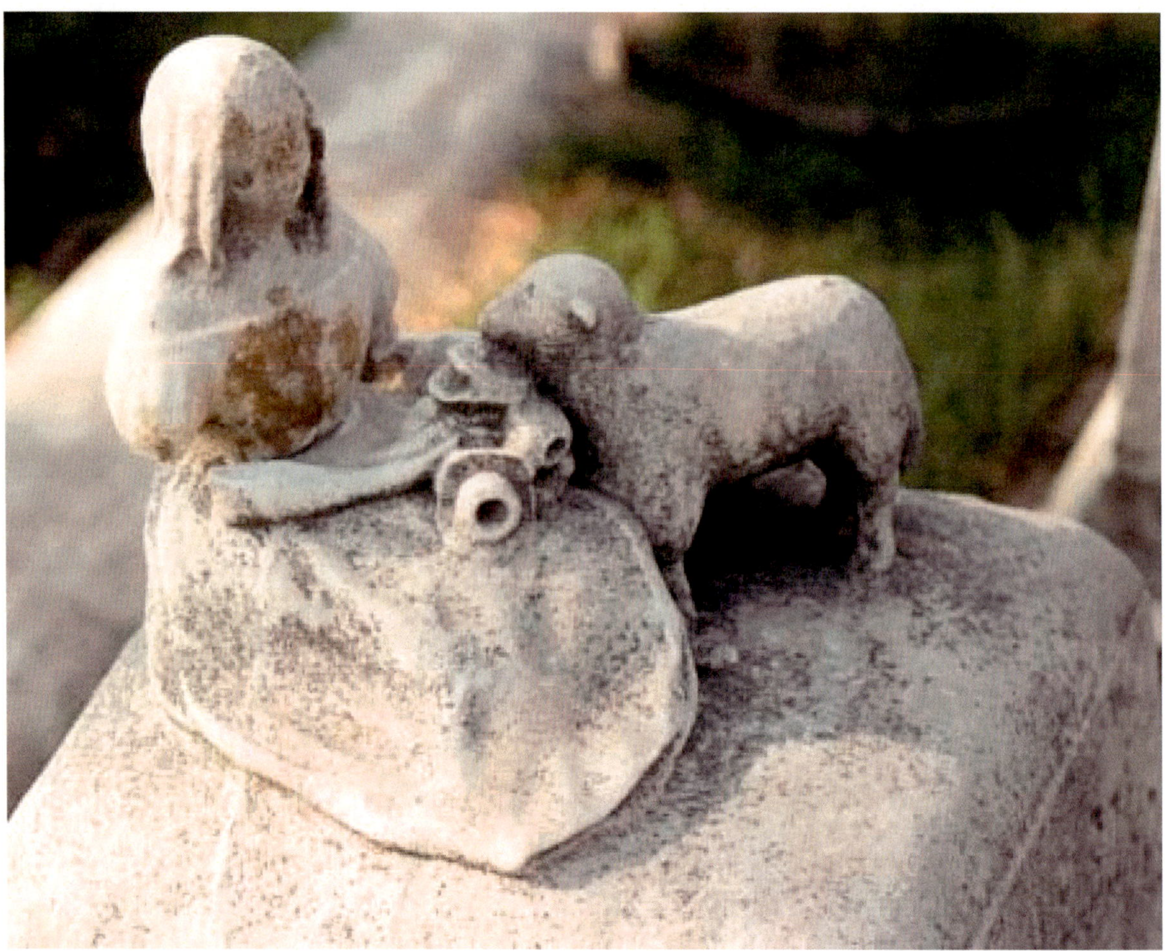

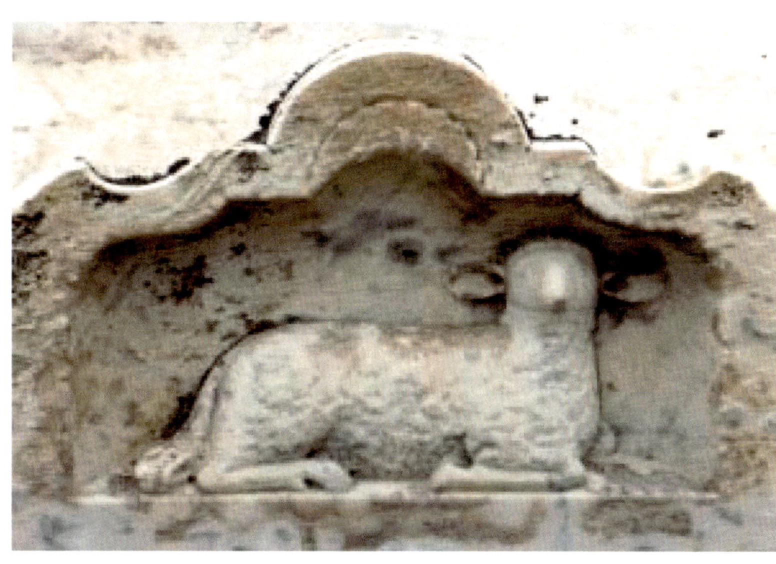

there may be a secondary reference to a shepherd as a symbol. A plethora of biblical references to lambs and shepherds can be found. Some of the most famous examples include Isaiah 40:11: "He tends his flock like a shepherd; He gathers the lambs in his arms and carries them close to his heart," and Micah 5:4: "He will stand and shepherd his flock in the strength of the Lord."

The New Testament contains references to Jesus as the Good Shepherd, and also to Jesus as the Lamb of God. For instance, John 10:11 and 10:14: "I am the good shepherd; the good shepherd lays down his life for the sheep," and "I know my sheep and my sheep know me." Other references include John 1:30: "And looking upon Jesus as he walked, he said, Behold the Lamb of God." Other biblical references to lambs, sheep, and shepherds include Ezekiel 34:23; I Peter 5:4; Hebrews 13:20; I Corinthians 5:7; Revelation 5:12 and 7:17.

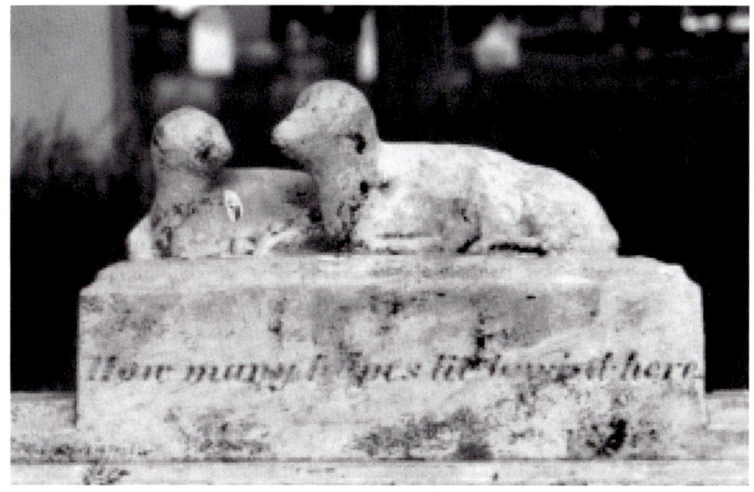

It was a common 19th century Christian belief that people were the sheep of Jesus's flock and that Jesus was the Good Shepherd. Not only was the symbol widely used on grave markers, it was even more widely used for stained glass windows in churches. Many churches were constructed with a "Good Shepherd" window over the altar. The lamb was a very familiar representation.

LAMP

For Christians. the use of a lamp as a symbol on a grave marker was a demonstration of spiritual comfort. The words in Psalm 119:105 are an example: "Thy word is a lamp unto my feet, and a light unto my path." This interpretation is supported in II Samuel 22:29: "You, Lord, are my lamp; the Lord turns my darkness into light," and Isaiah 62:1: "And for Jerusalem's sake I will not rest, until the righteousness thereof go forth as brightness, and the salvation thereof as a lamp that burneth."

The lamp can also represent the lamp of learning. In that context it was used on the grave markers of educated people, of teachers, and of people who loved to read.

Other instruments of lighting might be used for the same symbolic meaning. Thus there could be candles, lanterns, and other lighting devices although there are very few examples of these symbols on grave markers in Iowa or the Midwest.

Other relevant biblical references include Psalm 18:28 and Proverbs 20:27.

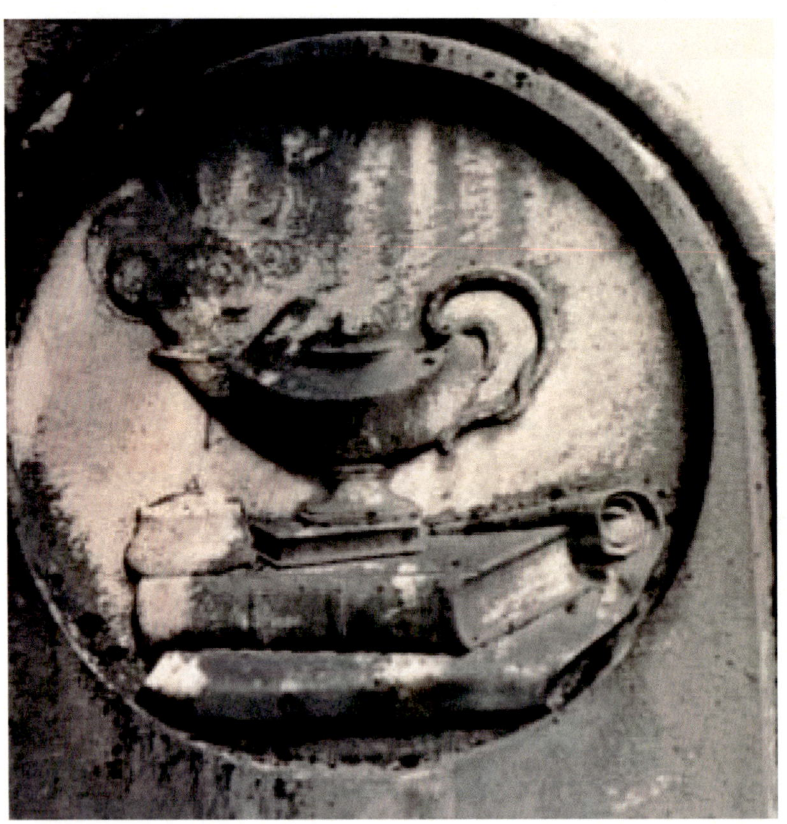

MOON

The moon is considered to be a heavenly body. When used on a grave marker, the moon is an indication that the soul of the person buried in this grave has gone to heaven. The moon often is used in conjunction with the heavenly gates and the heavenly city. The moon is the symbol of the Blessed Virgin Mary, and as such is considered a feminine symbol. When used by itself, the moon is most often found on the grave markers for women. When used with other symbols, this is not necessarily the case.

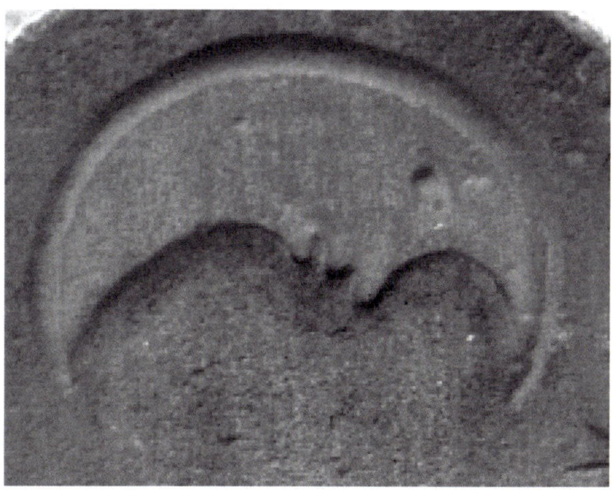

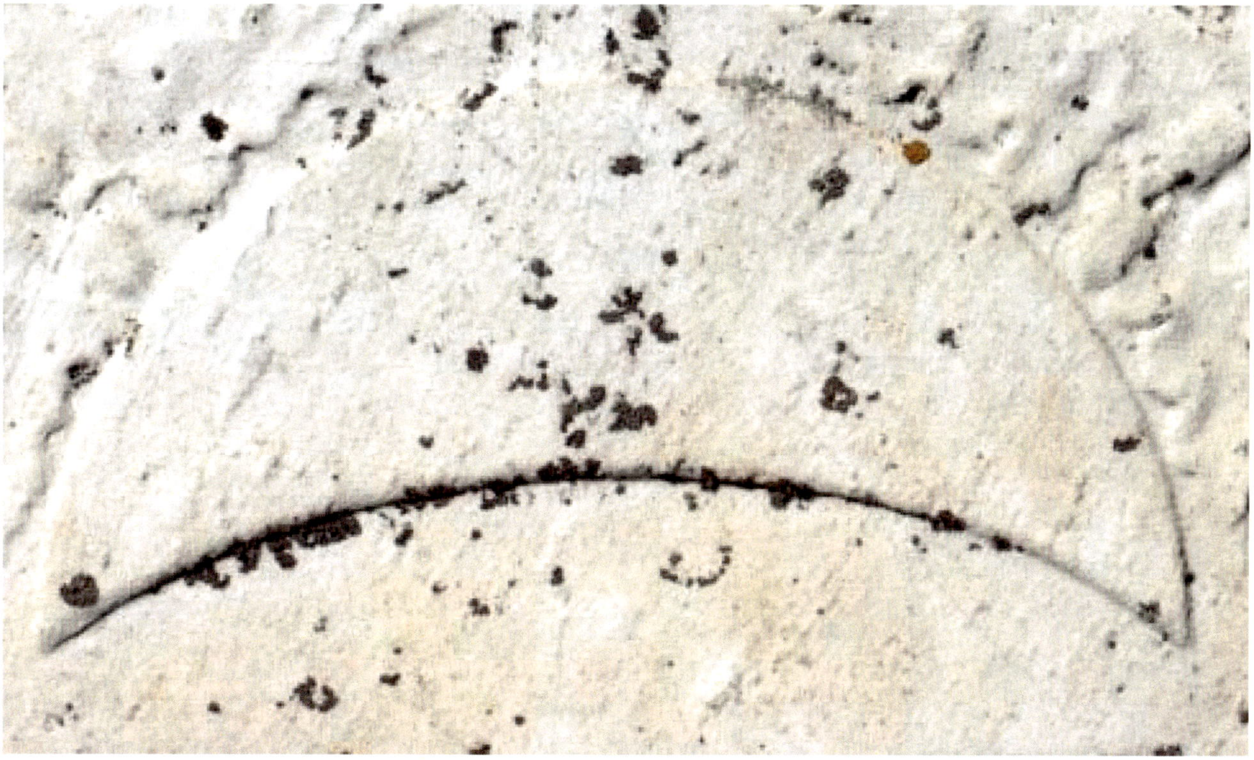

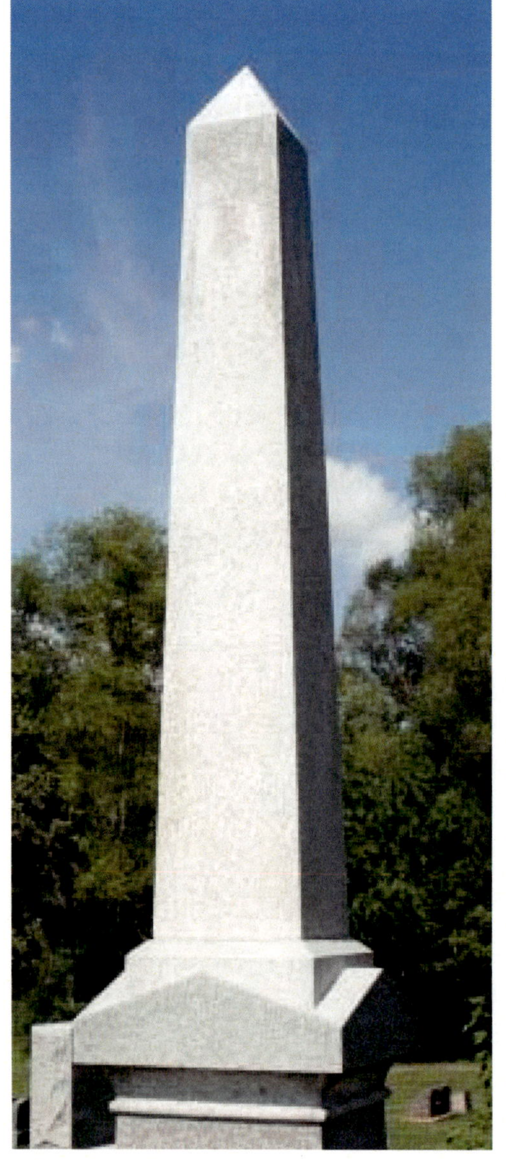

OBELISK

An obelisk is a square stone column which tapers to a point at the top. The word derives from the Greek *obeliskos*, which translates as "a needle or a pointed pillar." In the Latin *obeliscus*, the translation is "a small spit or leg of a compass." Obelisks were prominent in ancient Egyptian architecture where they usually were placed in pairs at the entrance of temples. After the Napoleonic wars in Europe, it became fashionable to imitate Egyptian art and architecture. This style also became popular in the United States during the 19th century. Perhaps because people associated the obelisk with death, tombs, and funerals, the obelisk became a common shape for grave markers throughout this country. Perhaps it would be more accurate to state that the obelisk was not a symbol on a grave marker, but rather the obelisk shape *was* the grave marker.

For the last two centuries many people have become fascinated with obelisks, pyramids, mummies, and other things associated with death in ancient Egypt. In several cases, the cemetery gates and tombs within cemeteries are designed in the Egyptian Revival style.

In the book *The Revival Styles in American Art,* by Peggy McDowell and Richard E. Meyer (Bowling Green, Ohio: Bowling Green State University Popular Press, 1994), the authors state: "The obelisk is one of the most pervasive of all the revival forms of cemetery art. There is hardly a cemetery founded in the 1840s and 1850s without some form of Egyptian influence in the public buildings, gates, tomb art, etc."

In the United States where obelisks are used as grave markers, the monuments vary in height from only a few feet to truly gigantic proportions. Usually the obelisks in cemeteries are constructed of several blocks of stone placed one atop another, rather than being made from one large piece of stone. There are several instances where the obelisk used as a grave marker also has other symbols carved on the four faces.

PALM BRANCH

The palm branch represents the triumph, the victory, and the martyrdom of Jesus. For Christians it represents the hope of salvation. Although the palm branch does not often appear on grave markers, except as ornamentation, the symbolic meaning is quite clear.

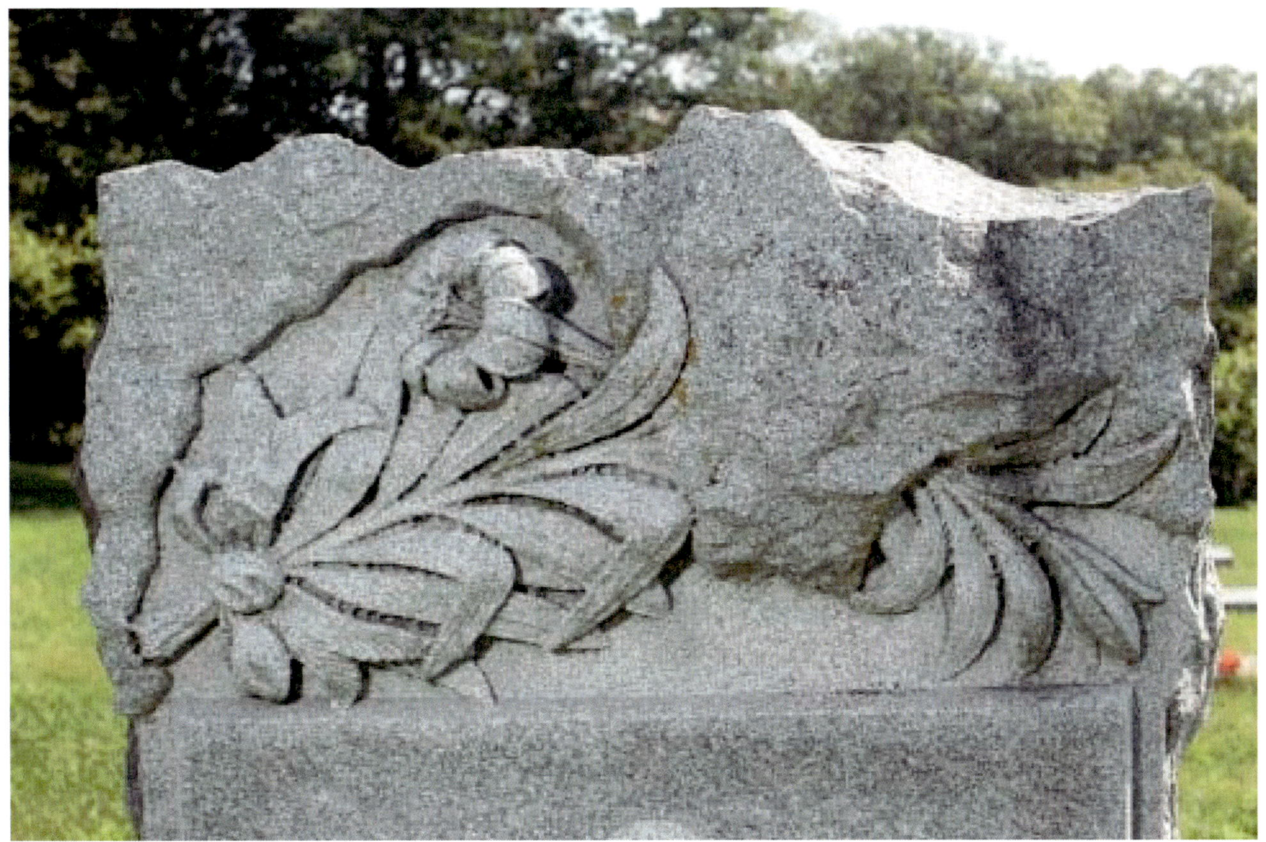

SCALES

An obvious meaning of scales as a symbol is the fact that scales are used for weighing. For Christians, the reference to weighing referred to a judgment by God, the balance of a person's good deeds versus the bad deeds. This is similar to the record of deeds kept in the Book of Life (see "Book of Life," page 22)

The usual feeling in the 19th century seems to have been positive; therefore, the scales would not be used on a grave marker unless survivors were convinced that the deceased had a preponderance of good deeds. In a sense, the scales meant a sort of reckoning at the time of the Last Judgment. Some individuals and some religious denominations believed the soul of the deceased was judged at the time of death.

The words of Job 31:16: ". . . let God weigh me in honest scales and he will know that I am blameless" help us to understand this symbol. Other helpful biblical references to scales include Proverbs 11:1, Daniel 5:27, and Revelation 6:5.

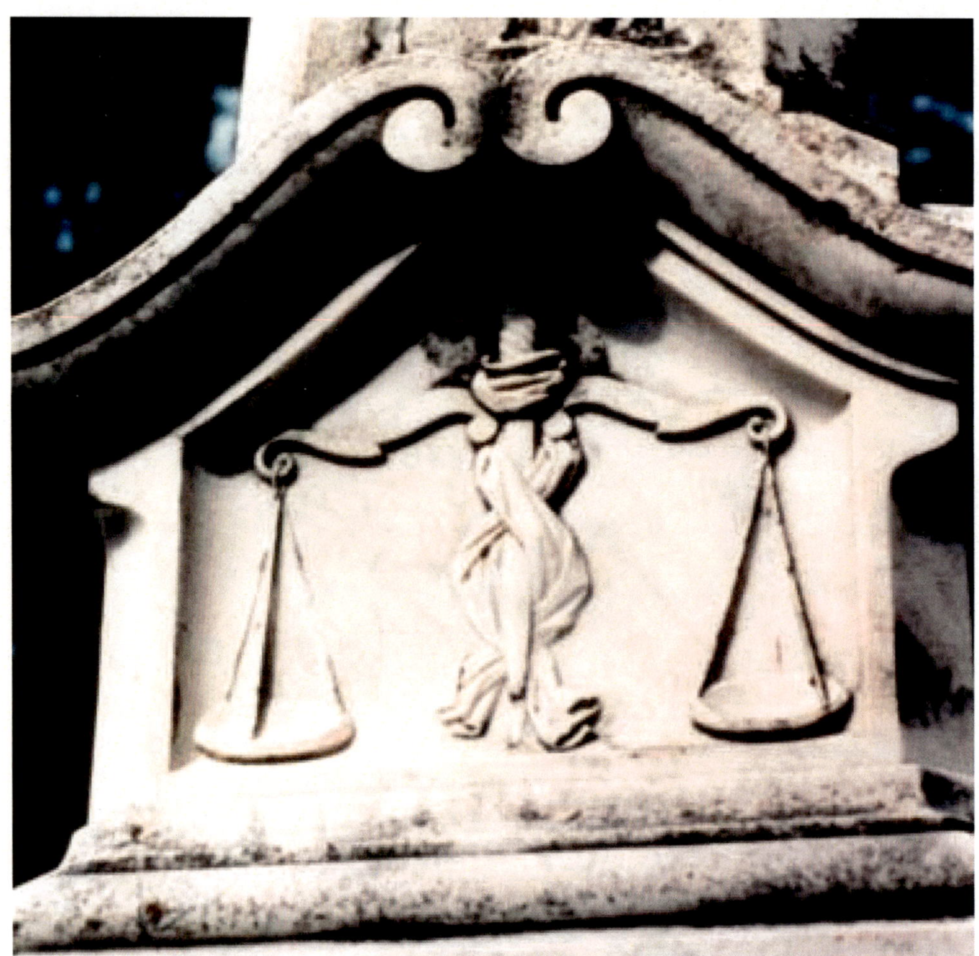

SCYTHE, SICKLE

The scythe or the sickle, common tools of agriculture, take on a new meaning when they are included as symbols on grave markers. Sometimes the two words are used interchangeably, but sometimes they are defined separately, both as tools and as symbols. During the Medieval period in Europe the scythe came to be thought of as the instrument of death, with death itself represented as a skeleton. The symbolic figure of death carrying a scythe also has been used on grave markers, although this image fell out of favor by the end of the 18th century and is rarely found in Iowa or the Midwest.

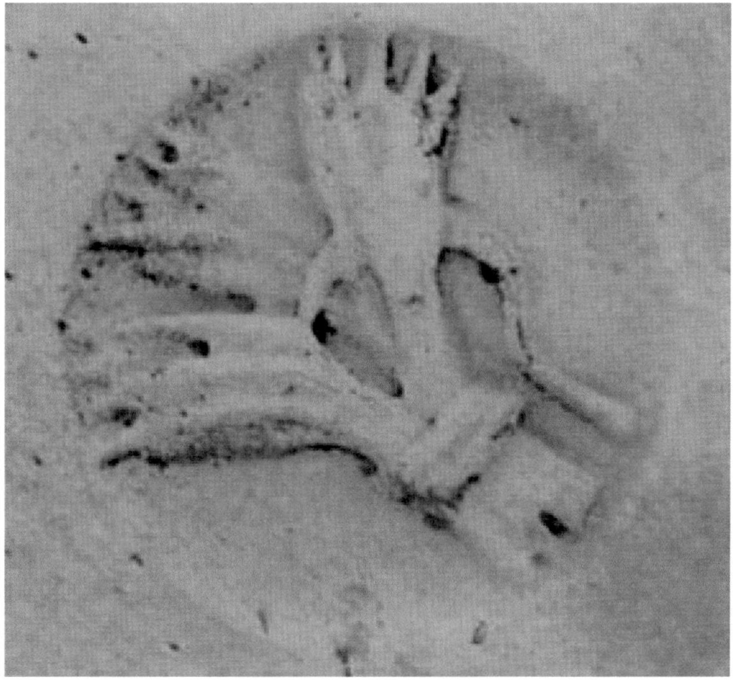

The sickle is the more common symbol on grave markers, representing the idea that the person whose grave is marked has lived a full life span of 70 years. The sickle seems to be more common on the graves of men than on the graves of women. Since the biblical span of life was 70 years, this symbol was considered to be appropriate for the grave markers of elderly men. The 19th-century idea was that a person who was older than 70 years was ripe and ready for harvest. Often the sickle is portrayed with a sheaf of wheat.

Revelation 14:15: "And another angel came out of the temple, crying with a loud voice to him that sat on the cloud, thrust in thy sickle and reap; for the time is come for thee to reap; for the harvest of the earth is ripe." Revelation 14:18: "Thrust in by sharp sickle and gather the clusters of the vine of earth; for her grapes are fully ripe." Joel 3:12-13: "Let the nations be roused; let them advance into the Valley of Jehoshaphat, for there I will sit to judge all nations on every side. Swing the sickle for the harvest is ripe." Mark 4:26-29: "He also said, This is what the kingdom of God is like. A man scatters seed on the ground. . . As soon as the grain is ripe, he puts the sickle to it, because the harvest is come."

SEA SHELL

Sea shells of various kinds were used as pre-Christian symbols of death. The shell is one of several pre-Christian symbols which were adopted by the Christians, sometimes with entirely different meanings. To people in ancient times, the shell was a symbol that while the physical remains of a person might be buried, the spirit of that person had gone elsewhere. To Christians the meaning was the same: the body is buried here, but the soul has departed. Just as a living creature once inhabited the sea shell, that creature is gone and only the dried remnant of the shell is left behind.

To Christians, the sea shell was also used as a symbol of baptism. There are many grave markers where the main symbol is the shell, but the effigy of the person memorialized is carved as resting within the shell.

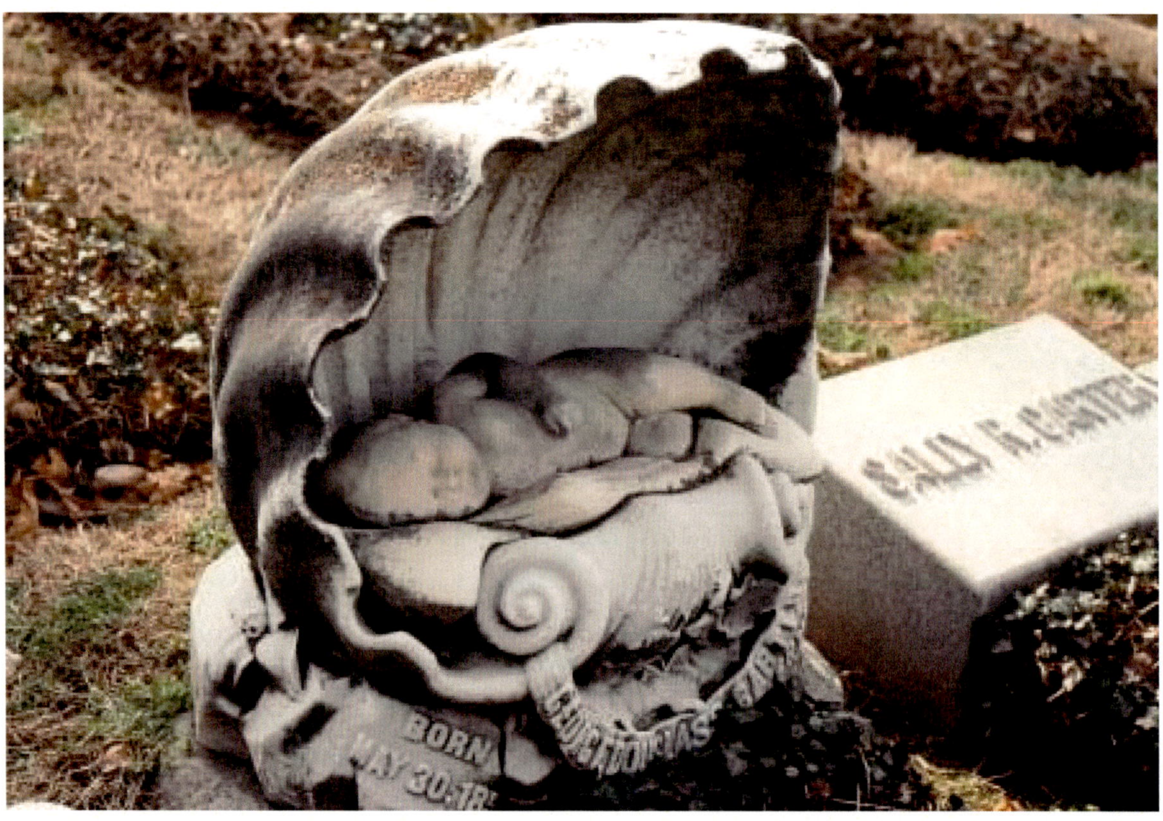

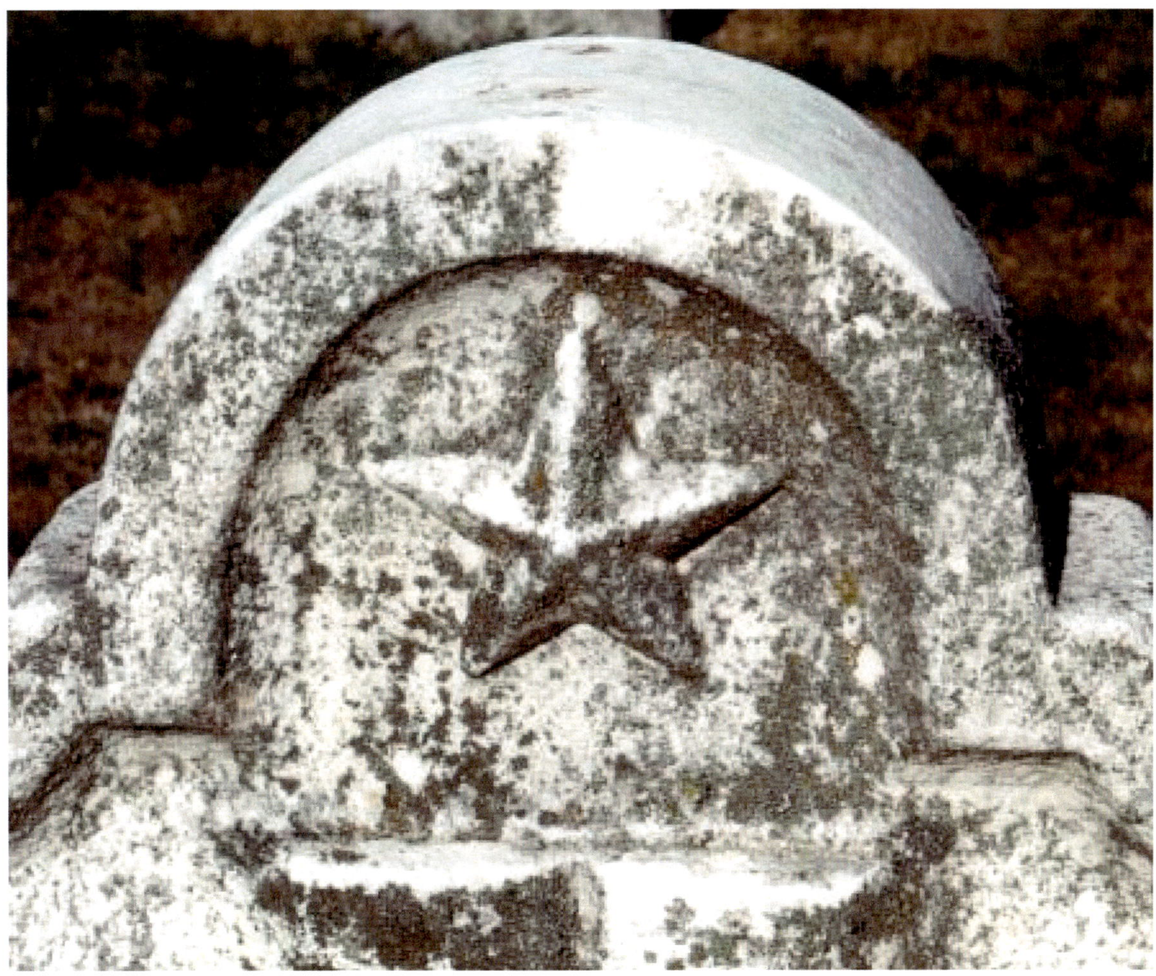

STAR

The star represents another heavenly body. During the 19th century, the star was considered to be a masculine symbol and might be used on the grave marker of a man. It was often carved above the heavenly gates and the golden stairway to heaven. The star also is a symbol of God's guidance to the true path of salvation. There is a difference of opinion among Christian denominations as to whether this idea stemmed from the star which appeared over Bethlehem at the time of the Nativity.

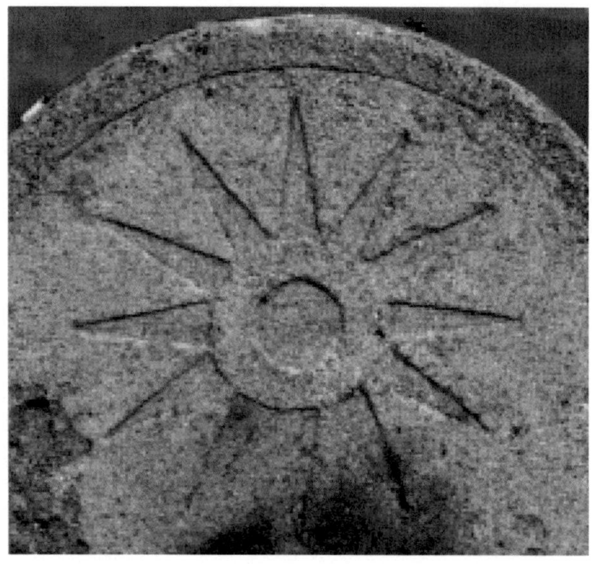

SUN

The sun is a heavenly body in the same sense as the moon is a heavenly body. The sun is a masculine symbol and ordinarily would be used on a grave marker for a man. The sun also appears over the heavenly city skyline as an indication that God is present in heaven. Sometimes the interpretation is enlarged to mean that God is the center of the universe, and that all life comes from God.

If the sun is portrayed as only partially visible over a horizon, people in the 19th century felt that this would mean a setting sun, that life on earth was over for the deceased person. On rare occasions the partial sun was interpreted as a rising sun, indicating that eternal life was beginning for deceased person.

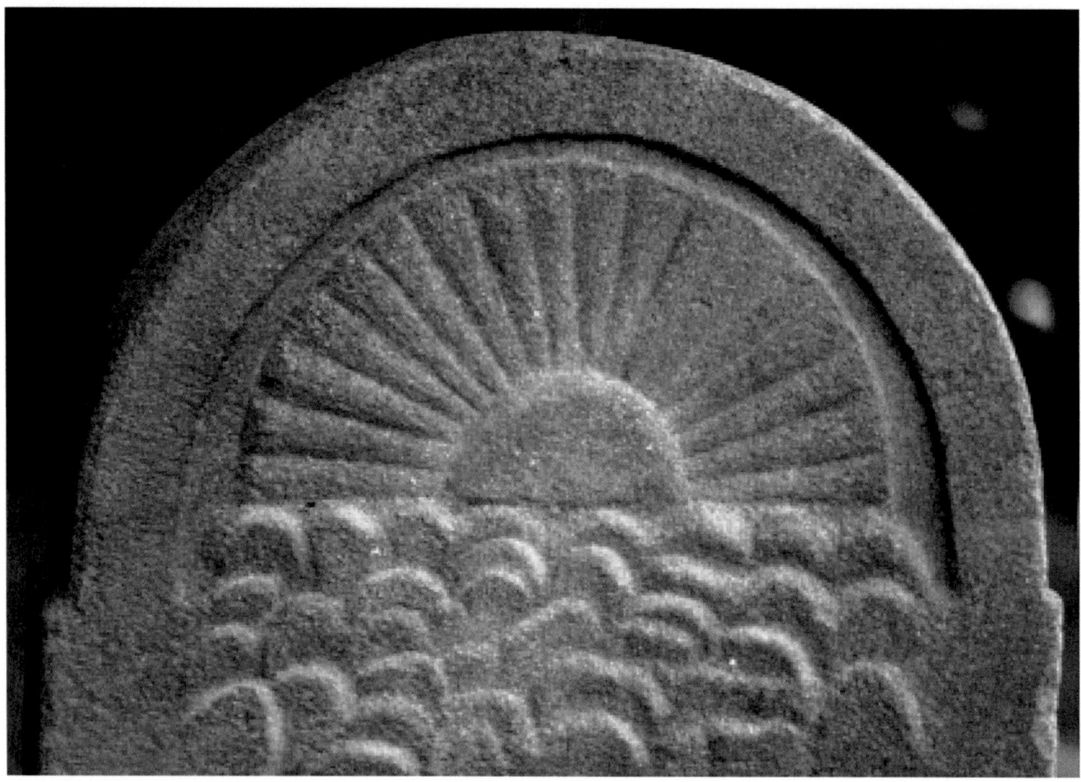

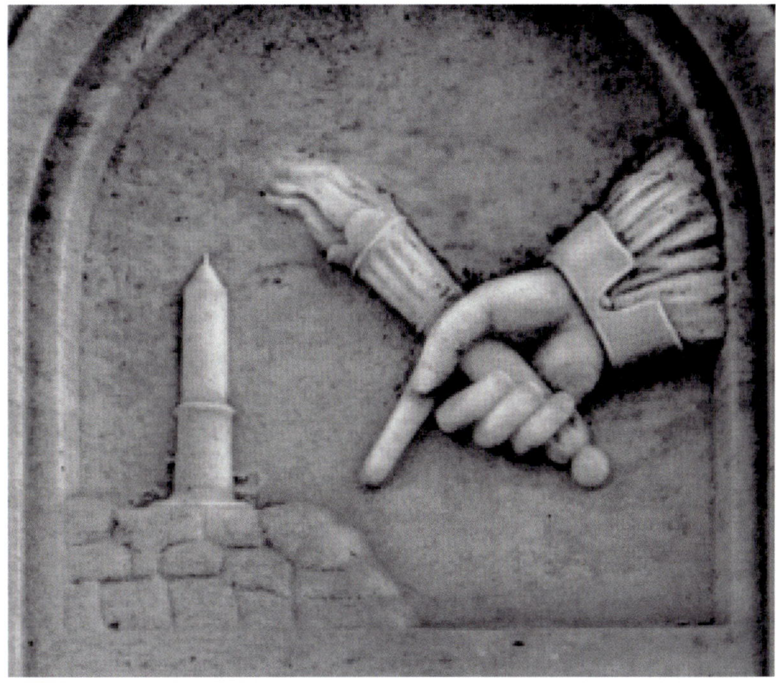

TORCH

The torch is an ancient symbol. Its use preceded Christianity by many centuries. The original meaning of the torch depended upon whether the torch was upright or inverted. An upright, lighted torch was the symbol of life. An inverted or upside down torch was the symbol of death. Sometimes the action of inverting a lighted torch and extinguishing the flame was an order for execution.

The Christian Church adopted the torch in both of its manifestations. On a grave marker, an inverted torch is a symbol of the end of life as we know it. But the continuing flame, even of an inverted torch, is a sign that the soul still exists in an afterlife or in heaven. An upright torch with a flame simply indicated immortality.

Often on grave markers a torch was carved in a horizontal position. It is possible that this might be used simply for decorative purposes, although the original meanings may still apply.

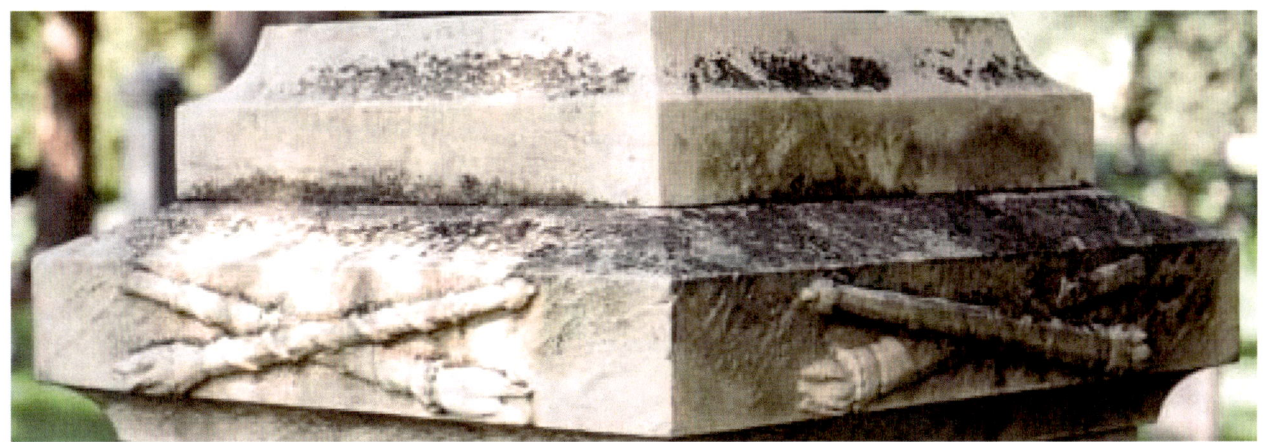

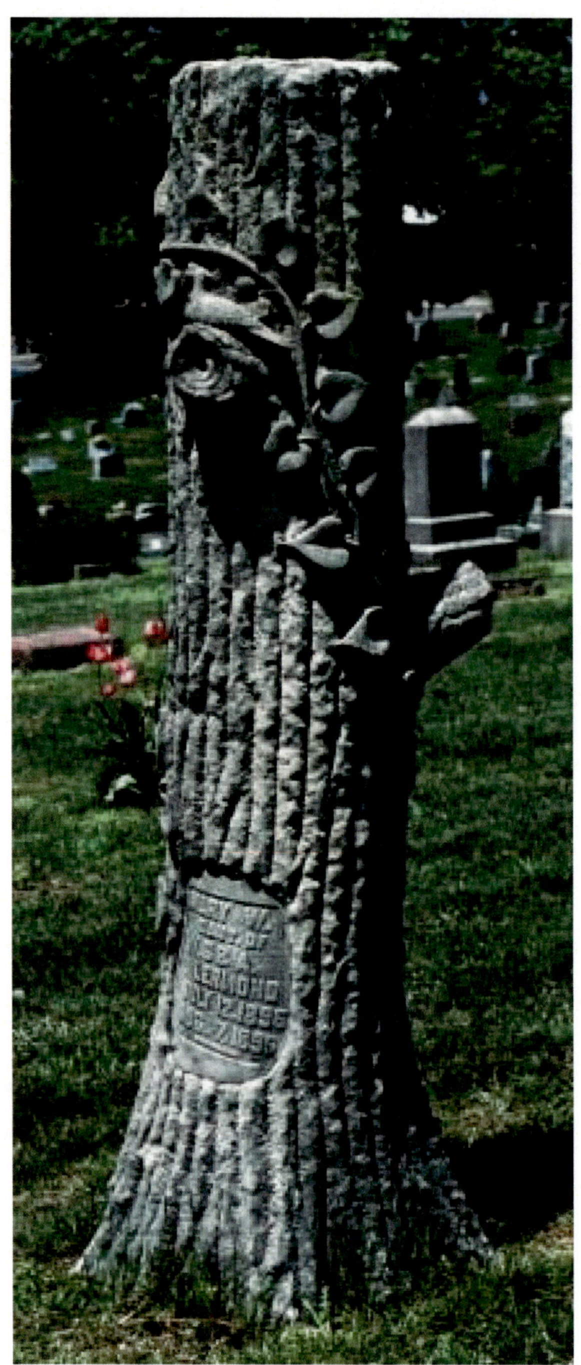

TREE STUMP OR TREE TRUNK

Stone carved into the shape of a tree stump or trunk was a common method of marking graves in the latter half of the 19th century and the early years of the 20th century. Several types of stone were used for these grave markers, but the best quality monuments were carved from oolitic limestone. (See "Oolitic Limestone," page 105) This material is found most abundantly in the Lawrence County, Indiana quarries. When first quarried the stone was easily carved, but when exposed to the air for a time and seasoned, it becomes much harder. Many grave markers carved from oolitic limestone show little weathering after more than a century of exposure.

There are several varieties and sizes of tree trunk grave markers. Some sources maintain that the number of branches cut off indicate the number of children in a family. There are examples of birds carved into the upper part of these markers, and other examples of dead birds carved at the foot of the markers. Quite often a fern or a potted plant was carved at the base of the tree stump.

There are examples where a branch is carved as if broken from the trunk of the tree. Technically this was supposed to mean the death of a child, but there are many examples where such a carving was simply a design element.

Because a tree stump or tree trunk is not

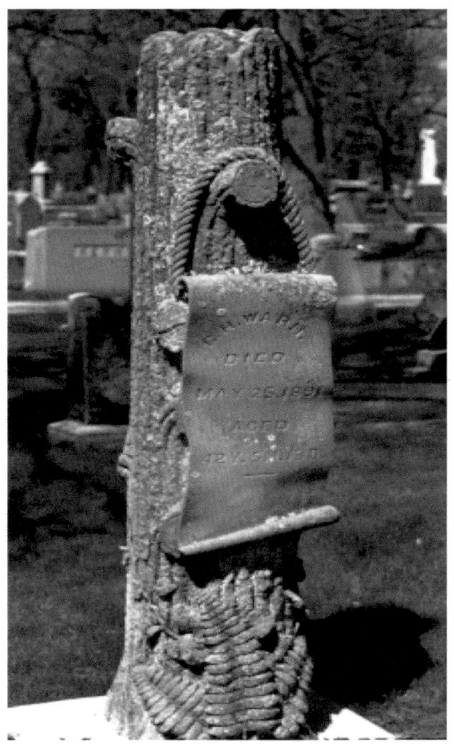

complete, it should logically have marked the grave of someone who had not reached the biblical span of three score and ten years. However this seems to have been ignored in a great many examples.

There are various methods of showing the information about the person whose grave is marked by these tree stumps. In some cases a section of bark is peeled back to provide a surface for the name and dates. In other cases a scroll suspended by a rope fulfills that purpose. Some tree stump markers have a shield carved in the surface for the name and dates.

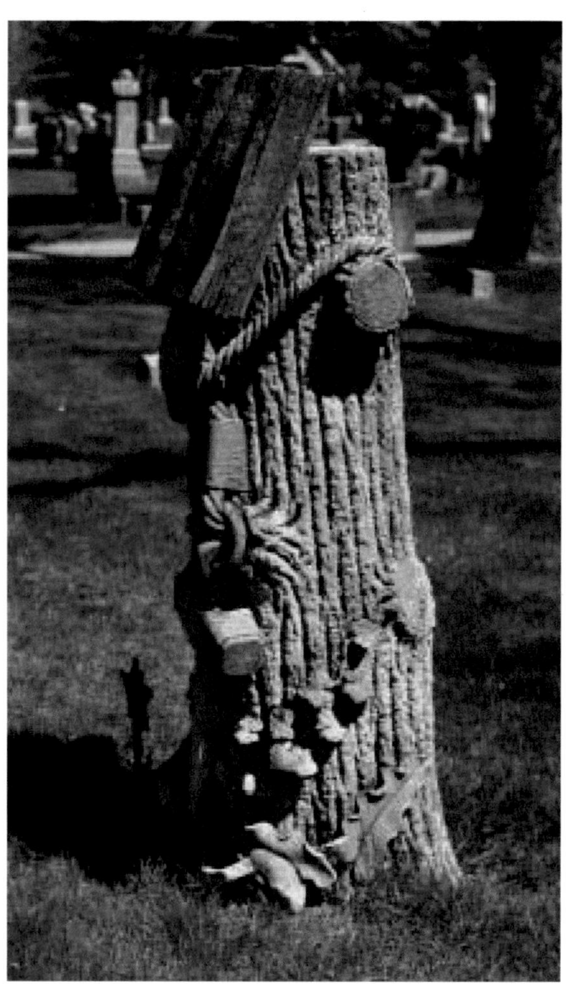

The tree stump grave marker was particularly favored by the Woodmen of the World lodge and the Modern Woodmen of America lodge. These two organizations helped members to purchase these markers, and because of the financial aid, many tree stump markers have the emblem of the lodge carved on them.

Oolitic limestone tree stump grave markers are very numerous in Iowa cemeteries and throughout the Midwest. Not all tree stump markers are on graves of members of the lodges mentioned. Most monument dealers were able to provide such grave markers for anyone who made the choice to purchase one.

TRUMPET

There are numerous references to trumpets in the Bible. Most often the references are to the day of judgment and the resurrection, and as a symbol on a grave marker this is the most common definition. Most likely it was an indication that people believed the soul of the deceased would be chosen at the last judgment. Only very rarely, and quite recently, would the symbol of a trumpet have had something to do with the musical ability of the person whose grave it marked.

A very commonly-known biblical reference to a trumpet is found in I Corinthians 15:52: "In a moment, in the twinkling of an eye, at the last trumpet; for the trumpet shall sound, and the dead shall be raised incorruptible, and we shall be saved." This verse became quite famous because it was used as one of the solos in the equally famous oratorio *Messiah*, by Georg Friedrich Handel.

Other biblical references include Revelation 11:15: "Then the seventh angel blew his trumpet, and there were loud voices in heaven, saying 'The kingdom of the world has become the kingdom of our Lord and of his Christ, and he shall reign forever and ever!" Matthew 24:31: "And he will send out his angels with a loud trumpet call, and they will gather his elect from the four winds, from one end of heaven to the other." I Thessalonians 4:16: "For the Lord Himself shall descend from Heaven with a shout, with the voice of the archangel, and with the trumpet of God; and the dead in Christ shall rise first. . . ." Isaiah 81:3: "All inhabitants of the world and dwellers on earth; when he lifts up a banner on the mountains, you see it; and when he blows a trumpet you hear it."

There are other possible interpretations of the trumpet symbol on a grave marker. Psalm 150:3: "Praise Him with the sound of the trumpet." Other biblical references include Isaiah 27:13, Joel 2:1, II Chronicles 20:28, and Revelation 11:15.

It is clear that the use of a trumpet on a grave marker may be interpreted as the symbol of the day of resurrection. It also is clear that it may be interpreted as a means of praising God. Either or both interpretations may have been intended when that particular symbol was used on a marker.

All of these biblical references to trumpets would have familiar to Iowans in the 19th century. There was even mention of trumpets in popular hymns. For instance, the first line of *When the Roll is Called Up Yonder* is "When the trumpet of the Lord shall sound and time shall be no more."

In spite of the large number of biblical references to trumpets, it is not a common symbol on grave markers in Iowa. Perhaps this is because it was so very difficult to carve a three-dimensional trumpet, and it was so very easy to damage such a marker.

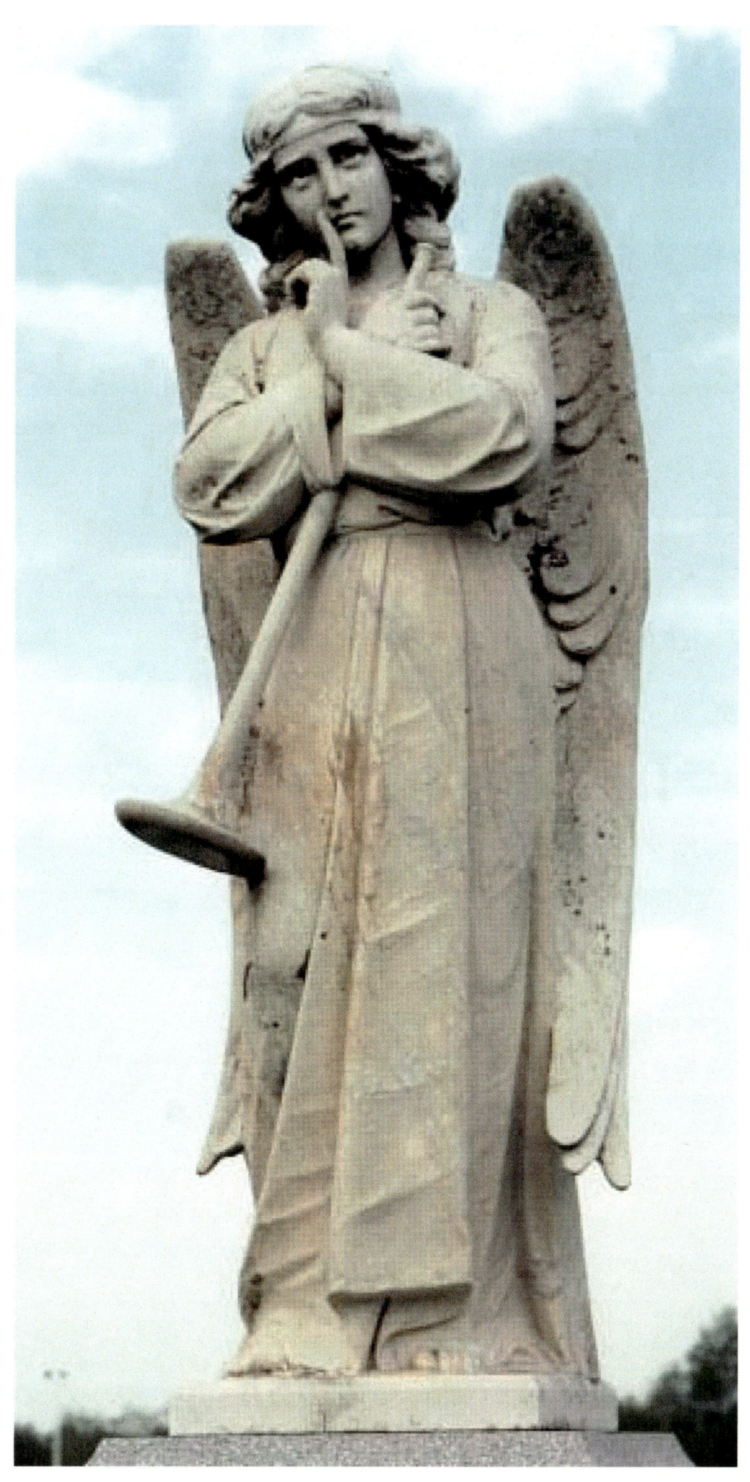

URN

Urns are common features in cemeteries, but for the most part they are not being used for the intended purpose. A funerary urn is a container for the cremated remains of a deceased person. But in earlier centuries, an urn sometimes contained body parts of a deceased person, particularly the heart. Sometimes the differentiation is made by calling the former "cinerary" urns and the latter "funerary" urns. This situation is complicated by the practice of using urns as decorations in cemeteries, either by themselves or as embellishment to other grave markers.

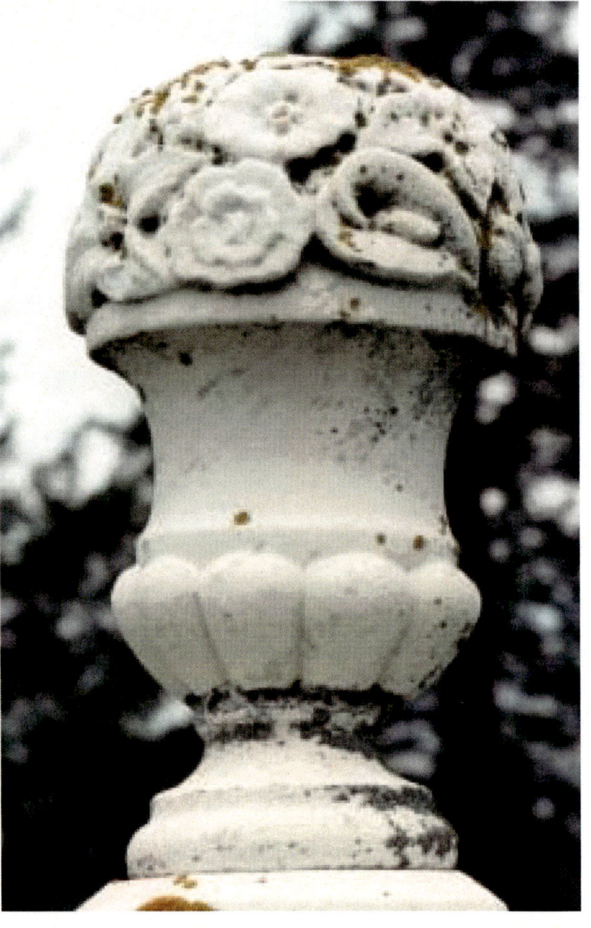

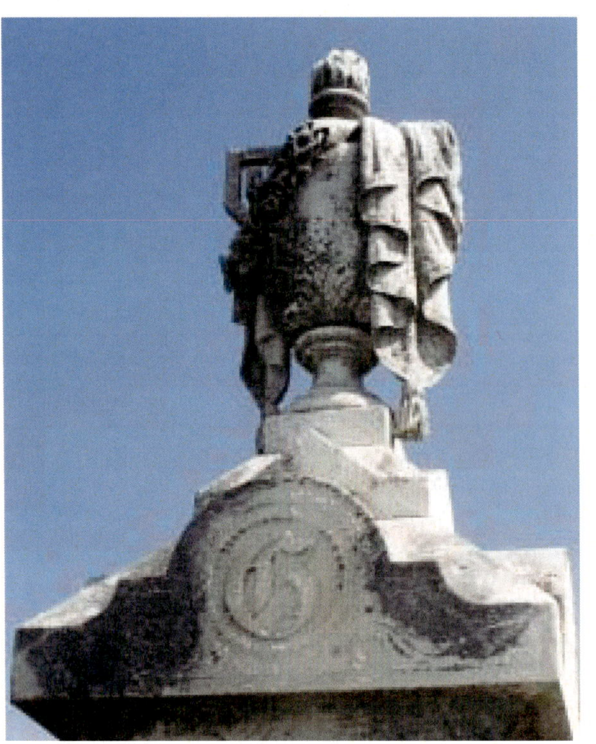

Urns were known in ancient times and were considered to be a symbol of death, as well as being used as a receptacle for the remains or portions of the remains of deceased persons. Christians adopted the urn for its practical function and also as a symbol that while the physical body remains, the soul has gone to heaven. On 19th century grave markers, urns tended to be vase-shaped, with a narrow neck above a rounded body. Quite often they had covers or lids. However, the body was solid; the urn was never intended to contain anything. Many white bronze grave markers had an urn on the top. Many stone shaft grave markers also had an urn on the top. In the latter case, the urns were secured in position with a pin, but over time a great many of the urns have become dislodged and no longer are with the original marker.

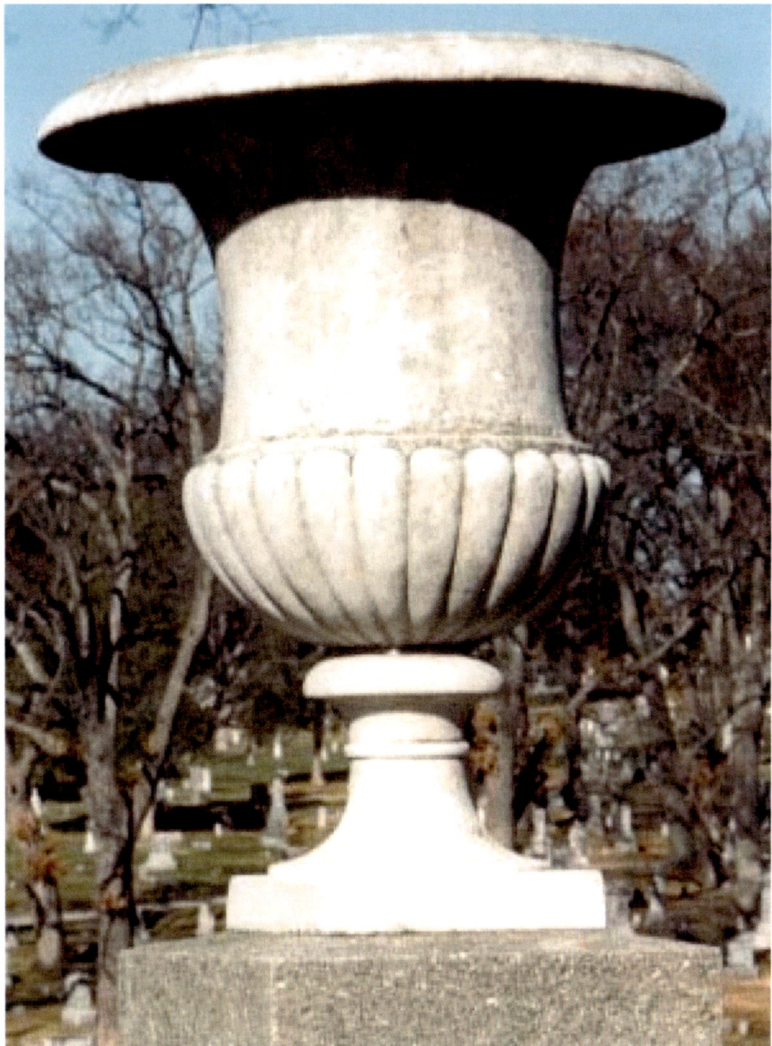

In many cases an urn on a grave marker is carved as though it was draped with cloth. The draped urn is simply an enhanced death symbol, because the drape represents the pall, the cloth which was used to cover coffins. This covering masked any ostentation that might attend decorated coffins and made all deceased persons appear equal in death.

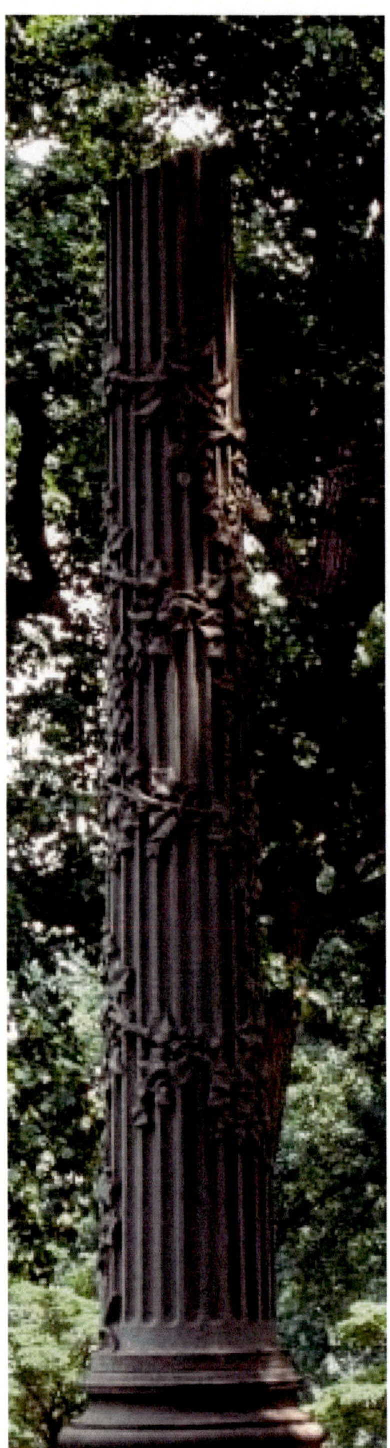

VINE

The vine is a symbol for the sustenance of spiritual life, provided by Jesus. It also represents the Holy Communion wine, almost certainly so if the vine is a grapevine. When used on a grave marker, a grape vine indicates that the person buried in this grave was in communicant status with a Christian church at the time of death. If the vine is ivy, then the meaning of the symbol is steadfastness of faith. The vine is also the symbol of ancient Israel and its people, who considered themselves to be God's "Chosen People." This is clearly presented in Psalm 80:8-9.

On a more individual basis, John 15:1 states, "I am the true vine, and my father is the gardener." John 15:5: "I am the vine; you are the branches. If you remain in me and I in you, you will bear much fruit."

In Iowa and in other Midwestern cemeteries, the vines portrayed on grave markers usually either are ivy or grape vines. However, stone carvers used vines as embellishments and ornamentations on grave markers, especially when creating borders. As in the case of the acanthus leaf, sometimes the carving is purely decorative and not representational.

WEEPING WILLOWS

The weeping willow tree is a recurring symbol on 18th and 19th century grave markers. Its scientific name is *Salix babylonica*, almost certainly derived from biblical references to the tree. Although the tree's place of origin was China, it now is common throughout Europe and North America. When coppiced or cut down, the weeping willow sends up numerous sprouts from its roots. That characteristic is why it was known as a symbol of rebirth or immortality in China. The tree was sacred to China, to Buddhists, and to the classical Greeks. Similar symbolic meanings about the willow tree were prevalent in Europe and North America, one of several reasons the weeping willow became a popular symbol on grave markers.

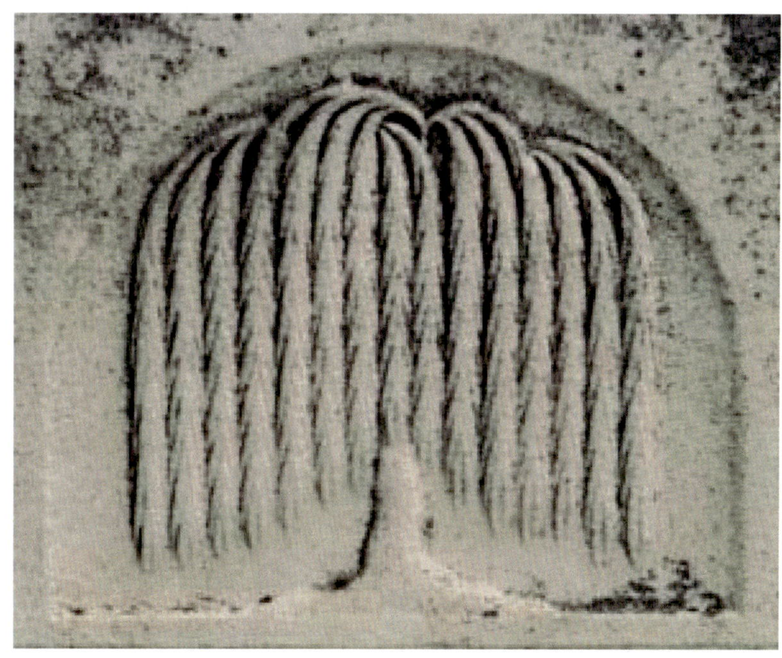

A common form of the symbol was a weeping willow overhanging an urn or a monument. In addition to symbolic meanings, the tree actually looked sorrowful. Even in Puritan New England this symbol was allowed because it could be used to further the idea of "*Memento Mori*." The Latin expression usually is translated as "Remember, you must die." The weeping willow overhanging the urn or monument became one of the most pervasive images in 18th century Puritan grave yards.

In Iowa and the Midwest the weeping willow on grave markers is not the most common symbol to be seen, but there are few cemeteries of any size that do not contain an example. The artistic renderings are varied, with a wide range of depictions of weeping willows on grave markers.

Weeping willow trees were often planted in cemeteries as landscape features. This also took advantage of another characteristic of the tree. Weeping willows have a strong and widespread root network which can absorb large quantities of water. Hence it was planted in low-lying or boggy areas of a cemetery to help absorb moisture and to prevent erosion of the soil.

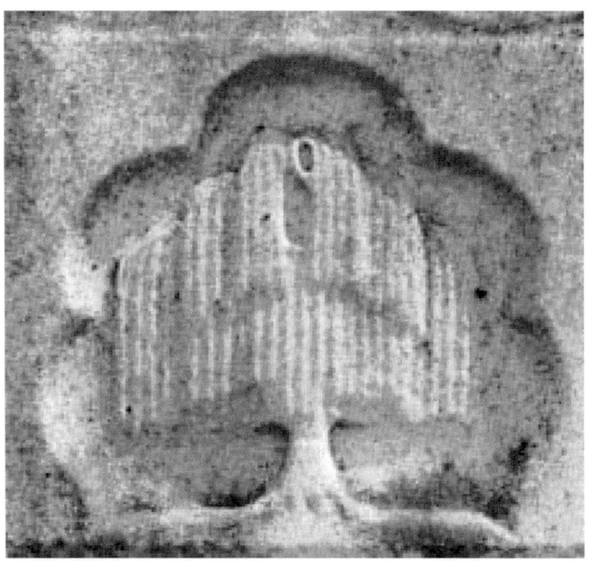

Numerous factors convinced 18th and 19th century Christians to use the weeping willow as a symbol on grave markers and, after 1831 when landscaping of cemeteries became more common, to plant the tree. Its name and its appearance seem sad. It offers hope of rebirth in a changed form. It functions well in wet areas of a cemetery. Most people admire its appearance and the shape and color of its leaves.

There is a famous biblical reference to willows, Psalm 137:1: "By the rivers of Babylon, there we sat down, yea, we wept, when we remembered Zion. We hanged our harps upon the willows in the midst thereof." Recent translations of the Bible insist that the proper name of the tree in this verse is poplar. But Iowans in the 19th century commonly used the King James translation of the Bible. They would not have been familiar with any other word than "willow" in that passage of the Bible.

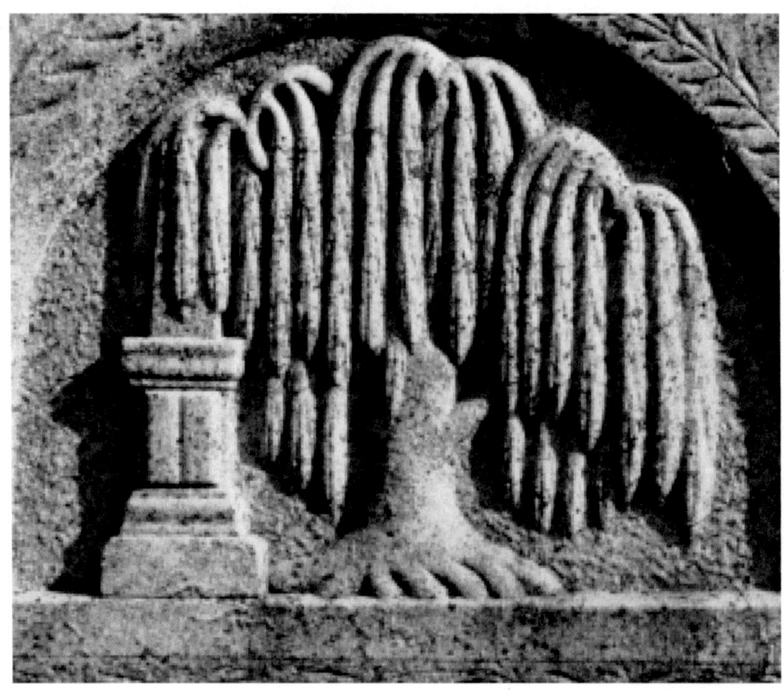

WHEEL

Circles and spirals have been common designs since prehistoric times. Often circles and spirals have sacred connotations. This practice has continued in the design and carving of grave markers. Few grave markers actually are circular in shape, but from the 17th century on in the United States, the circle has often been used as a design element.

During the 17th century in New England when Puritans tried to deny the use of symbols on grave markers, stone carvers added what were called "rosettes." These small, stylized circles were used on borders and to divide sections of markers. There is no evidence that the rosettes had particular meaning, but the fact they were called rosettes seems to show at least a tentative relationship to roses. Rosettes commonly were carved on the upper corners of Puritan grave markers.

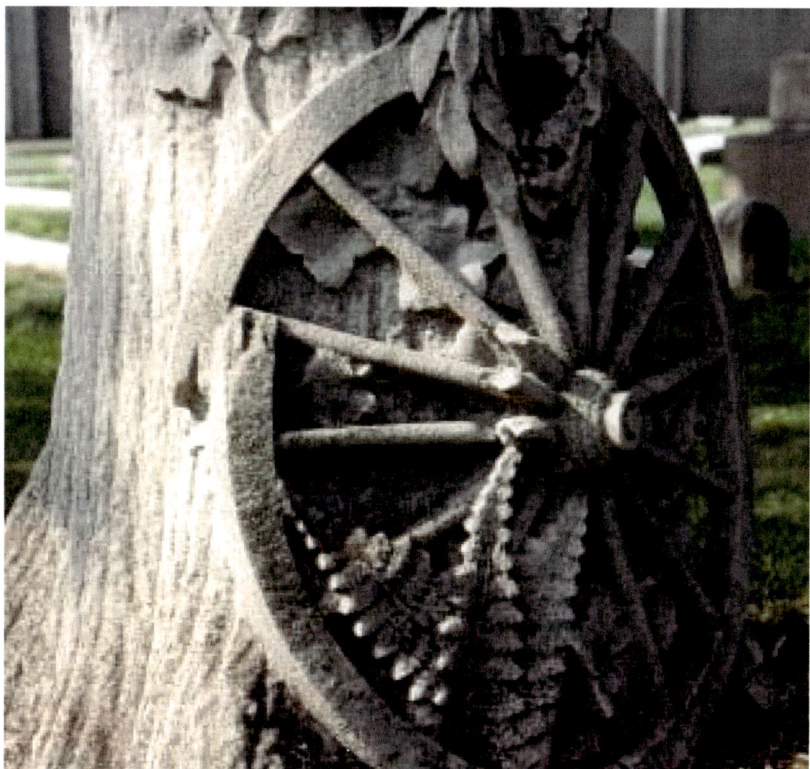

The use of the wheel offers a symbolic interpretation. Although not common, a few examples of this symbol do appear on 19th-century grave markers in the Midwest. The wheel symbolizes old age, a continuity of life. Often the wheel is portrayed as broken. To the people at that time, anything that was broken was a symbol of death, usually a death prior to age 70. When a wheel is used as a symbol on a grave marker, the rim is broken, and often one or more of the spokes also are broken.

There is a biblical reference to the wheel. Ecclesiastes 12:5-7, ". . . because a man goeth to his everlasting home, and the mourners go about the streets; before the silver cord is loosed, or the gold bowl is broken, or the pitcher broken at the fountain, or the wheel broken at the cistern, and the dust returneth to the earth as it was, and the spirit returneth unto God who gave it."

WREATH

The wreath is one of the simplest of all symbols on grave markers to interpret. Wreaths consist of multiple blooms of flowers or leaves of plants. Each flower and each leaf has its own meaning, so the collective definition of the wreath is the meaning of all of the flowers and leaves added together.

Wreaths composed entirely of one flower or leaf may have a more specific meaning. If the wreath is composed of laurel leaves, it was intended to mean victory. In classical Greece, there were regular gatherings for games and competition. Most people have heard of the Olympic Games, but the Pythian Games, dedicated to Apollo, were as famous then, and the winners were awarded a wreath of laurel. The classical Romans also awarded wreaths to winners, although those wreaths might be of gold. The Romans also awarded wreaths of laurel and oak.

There are very few biblical references to wreaths. I Corinthians 9:25 does mention winning in games. II Timothy 2:5 mentions winning athletes.

It is possible that during the 19th century, when furnishing a home meant over-furnishing it (to our taste), people thought wreaths and vases of flowers and baskets full of plants were appropriate. Survivors were surrounding the deceased family members with the type of furnishings familiar in homes.

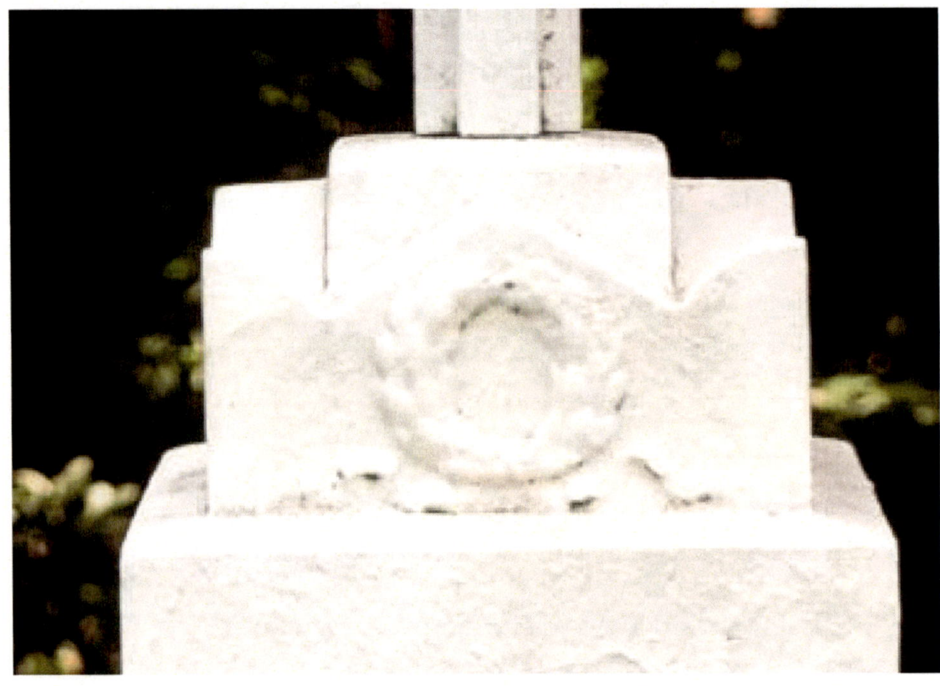

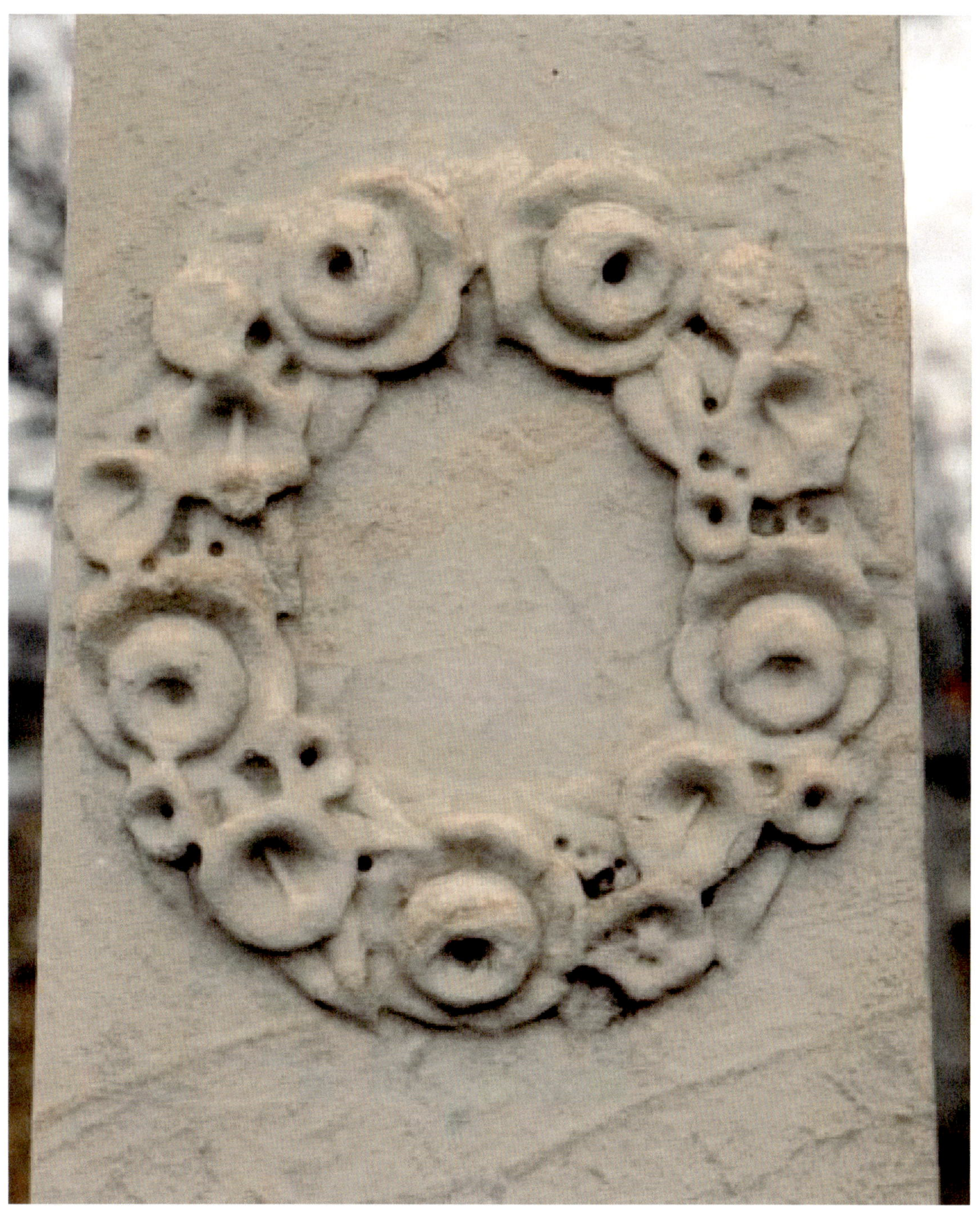

THE LANGUAGE OF FLOWERS AND LEAVES

Before the time when the population was generally literate, people had other means of communication. For instance, in ancient Persia and the eastern Mediterranean region there was a language of flowers, plants, and trees. This custom was adopted by Europeans and became quite sophisticated during the 19th century. It was most common when expressed with flowers and herbs, but meanings also were given to trees, leaves, and bushes. This language was known formally as "floriography" and became quite complex.

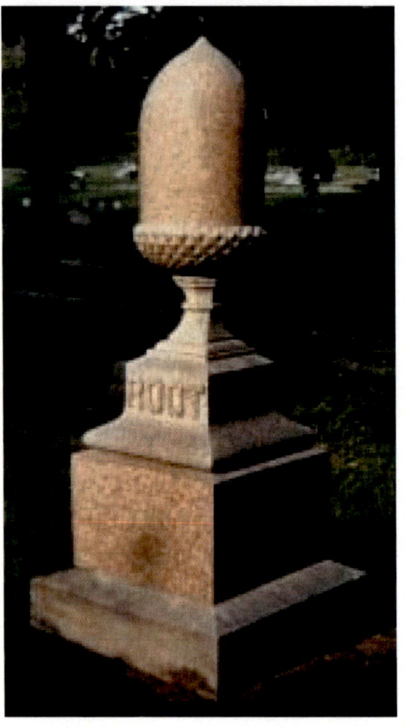

The custom of using flowers as a language and a means of communication became so popular that by the middle of the 19th century there were hundreds of publications devoted to the subject, in the languages of various countries. Some commonly-held definitions were established by two early 19th-century books, *Dictionaire du language des fleurs* (1809), by Joseph Hammer-Pugstall, and *La Language des Fleurs* (1819), by Louise Cortambert.

In the United States the best-known manifestation of this phenomenon was the publication of *The Old Farmers' Almanac,* beginning in 1792 and continuing to the present day. Within this almanac were lists of the meanings of various flowers, plants, and trees. Because of the extremely widespread distribution of this almanac, it is probable that knowledge of this language of flowers was known to the majority of the population of Iowa, the Midwest, and the United States. Distribution of *The Old Farmers' Almanac* reached more than 225,000 by 1863. Many, if not most, households in this country would have had possession of or access to a copy.

[The almanac was first known as *Farmers' Almanac*; the name was changed to *Old Farmers' Almanac* in 1832. It reverted to *Farmers' Almanac* in 1836 but was changed permanently to *Old Farmers' Almanac* in 1848.]

Most of the definitions or meanings given in the almanac were for flowers, but also included were the meanings of other plants: arbor vitae (friendship), ivy (continuity), oak (strength), pine (humility), and willow (sadness).

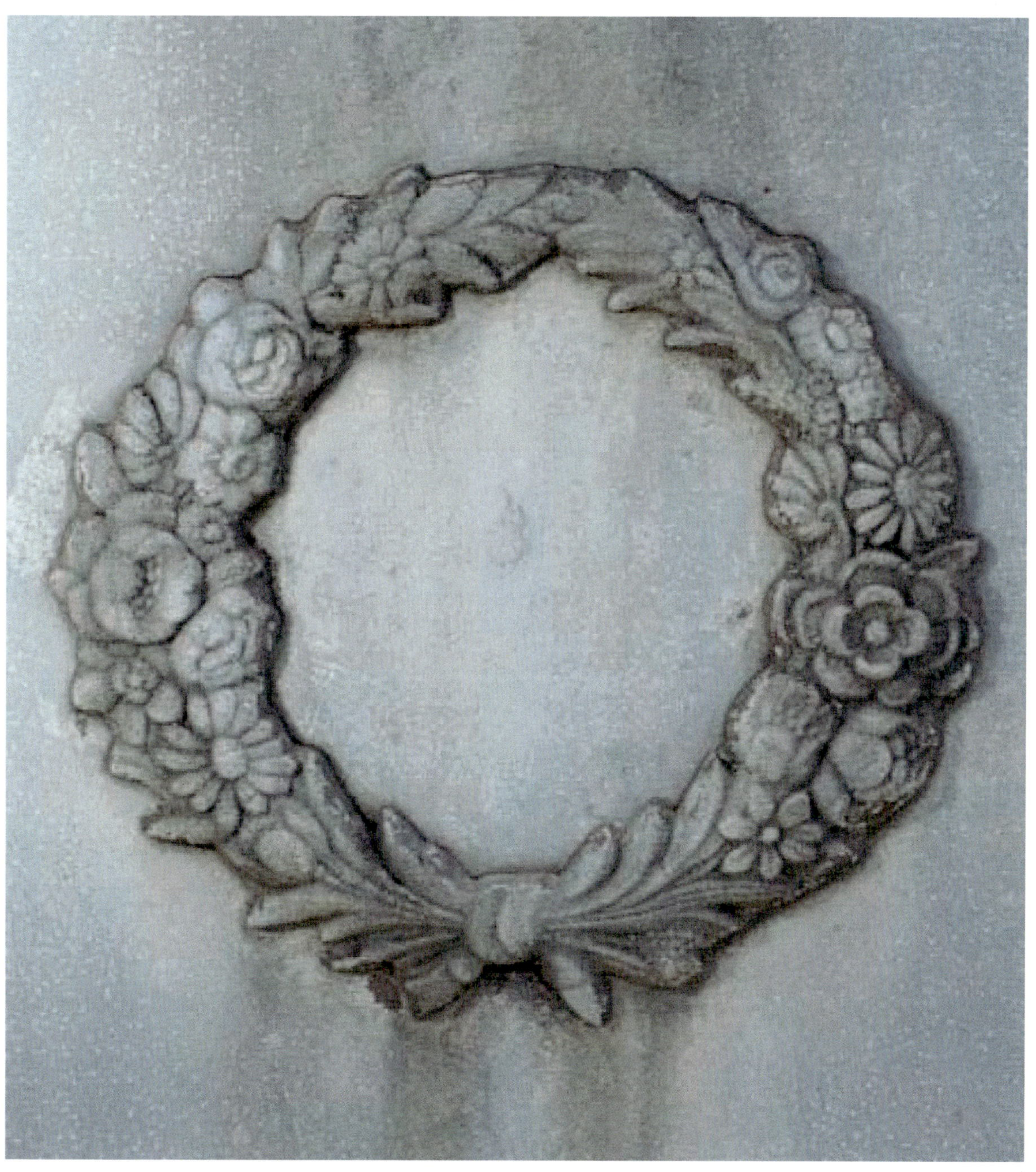

Literally dozens of almanacs and guide books to the language of flowers were published in the United States during the latter half of the 19th century. Not all of them were in agreement on the meanings of various flowers. But the circulation of *The Old Farmers' Almanac* greatly exceeded that of any other publication, so we may assume that more people were aware of the definitions contained therein, and that those definitions were better-known than the definitions of any of the competitors.

During the 19th century there also was a means of understanding the uses of and the meanings of plants, called "Doctrine of Signatures." This was an ancient idea, known as early as Galen but popularized by Jakob Bohme (1575-1624). The belief was that God marked objects with His "signature," indicating the purpose for each plant. This idea was a very human-centered concept, that the shape of a plant indicated which part of the human body that plant might be used to help or cure.

Before scientific knowledge was widely known or accepted, many people were willing to use particular plants not only to cure illnesses but symbolically to represent the causes of illness and death. There is at least the possibility that such beliefs may have carried over into the choices of symbols that were used on grave markers.

Some flowers and leaves were carved in such a stylized design that the true botanical species may not be apparent. It is also true that flowers and leaves were used on grave markers as ornamentation and borders, and in those cases no symbolic meaning may have been intended.

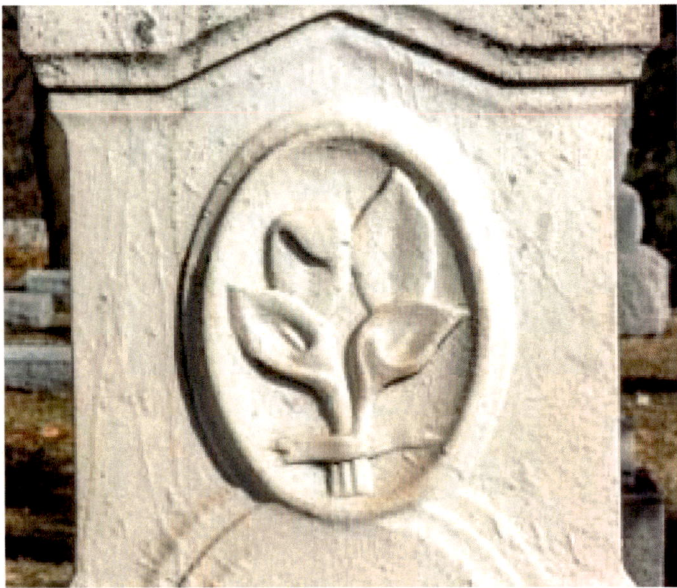

DAISY

The daisy meant simplicity.

HAWTHORNE

The hawthorne blossom was the symbol of home.

LILY

There are various kinds of lilies. The general meaning of any lily is purity and innocence. Also, the lily can be used to indicate humility.

Many lilies on grave markers are for the deaths of babies or infants, although they also are used for adolescent and unmarried females. The lily is rarely used on the grave markers of males over the age of five.

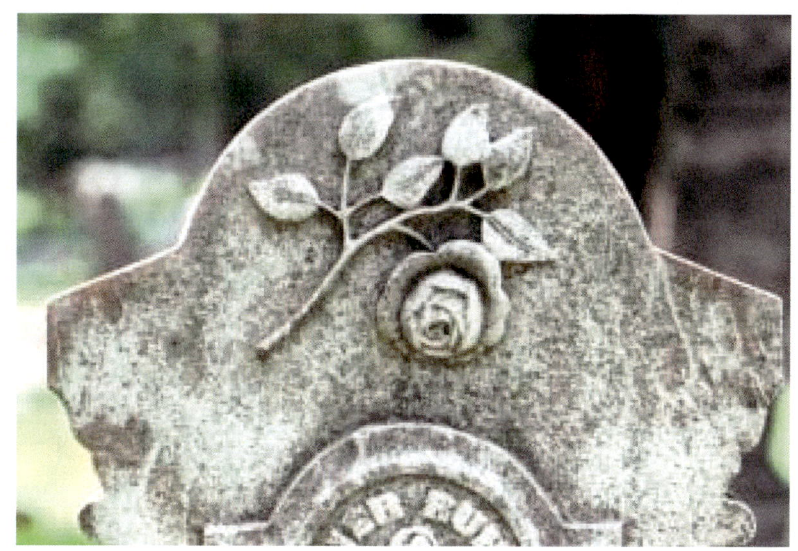

LOTUS

The lotus meant regeneration or immortality.

MORNING GLORY

The morning glory meant resurrection.

ORANGE BLOSSOMS

An orange blossom meant purity. This same symbolism applied to Victorian wedding bouquets.

ROSE

The rose is one of the most common flowers to be found on grave markers, occurring in the 18th, 19th, 20th, and 21st centuries. The meaning has remained constant. The rose meant love and beauty. In its full bloom form, it was used on the grave markers for adult females. As a rose bud, it was used on the grave markers of infants and very young children. A full-bloom rose with a rose bud on a marker usually meant that a mother was buried there together with her infant child.

The rose and the rose bud are each found in conjunction with other symbols. Roses may appear grouped in bouquets or in baskets, carried in the beak of a dove, shown with a broken stem, etc. In its stylized form, the rose may be used to decorate grave markers that are otherwise devoid of symbols. In that case it may have no symbolic meaning and simply be carved as an ornamentation.

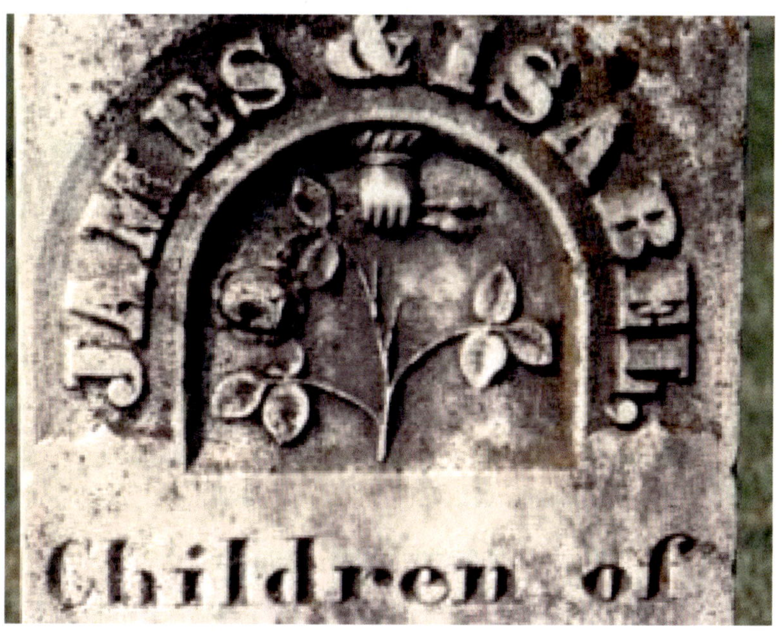

WHITE CAMELLIA

The white camellia meant perfect loveliness.

CEDAR OR OTHER EVERGREEN TREES

Any evergreen tree symbolized immortality. Not only were evergreens appropriate symbols on grave markers, they also were common planting in cemeteries. The evergreen tree ordinarily does not shed its needles, so it was an obvious choice to indicate everlasting life. The cedar tree also indicated steadfastness of faith, apparently because of the relative permanence of its form.

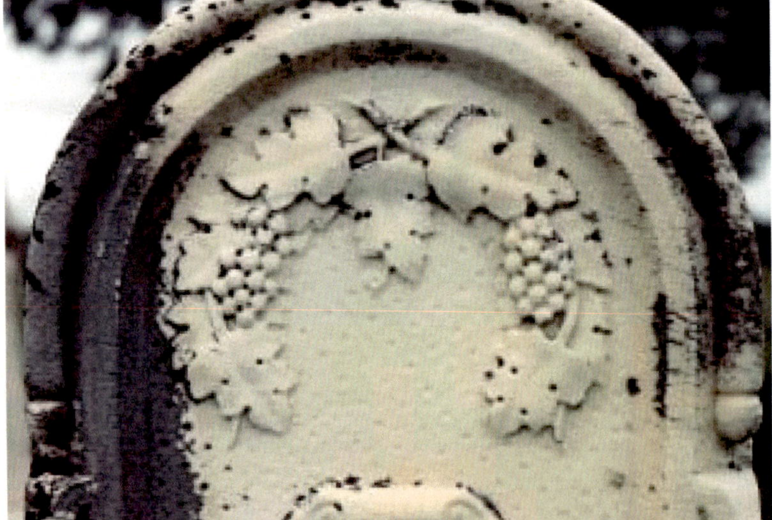

GRAPE LEAF

The grape leaf, particularly in conjunction with a bunch of grapes, represented the wine at communion. It also meant that the deceased person was mature in years.

IVY LEAF

The ivy leaf meant steadfastness, particularly of faith. (See photo page 58)

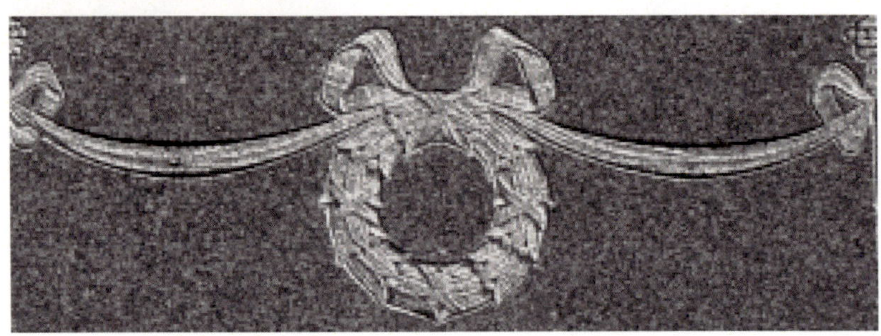

LAUREL LEAF

The laurel leaf is an ancient symbol of victory. In Christian terminology, its use on a grave marker meant the victory of eternal life over death. The laurel leaf usually was found carved in bunches or in wreaths, from the older custom of crowning the winners in contests with wreaths of laurel.

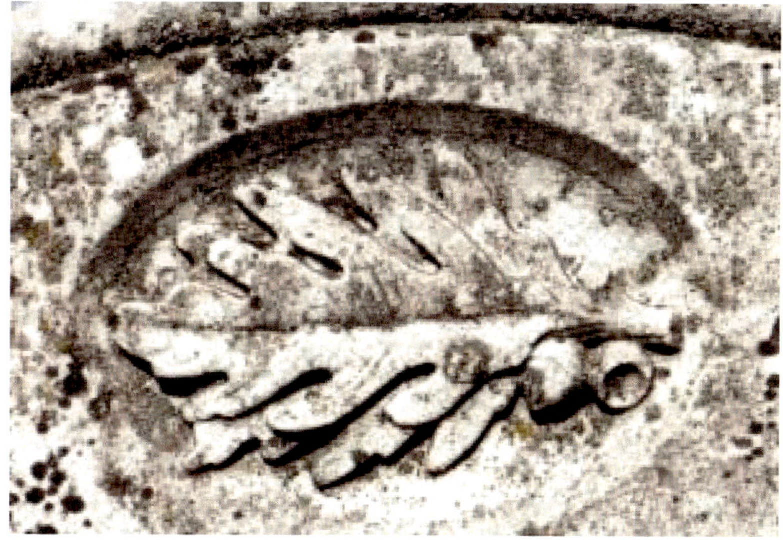

OAK LEAF

The oak leaf meant strength, particularly of faith. It was considered to be very appropriate on the grave markers of adult males. Biblical passages which mention the strength of oak trees include Genesis 35:8, Joshua 24:26, I Chronicles 10:12, and Amos 2:9.

PALM FRONDS OR BRANCHES

The palm branch represented the triumph, victory, and martyrdom of Christ. For Christians it meant the hope of salvation.

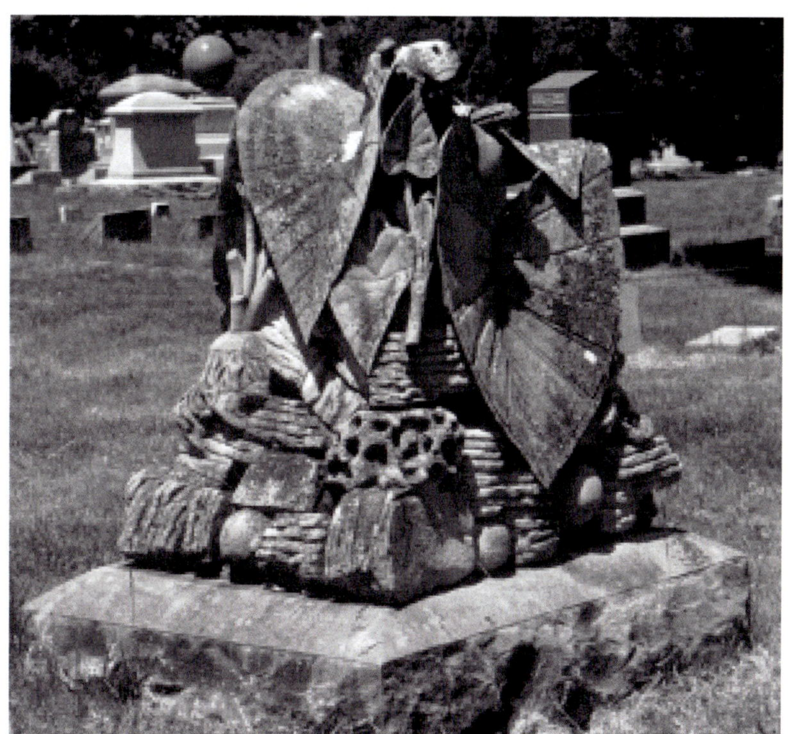

Please note references to other flowers, leaves, and trees under separate headings in this book.

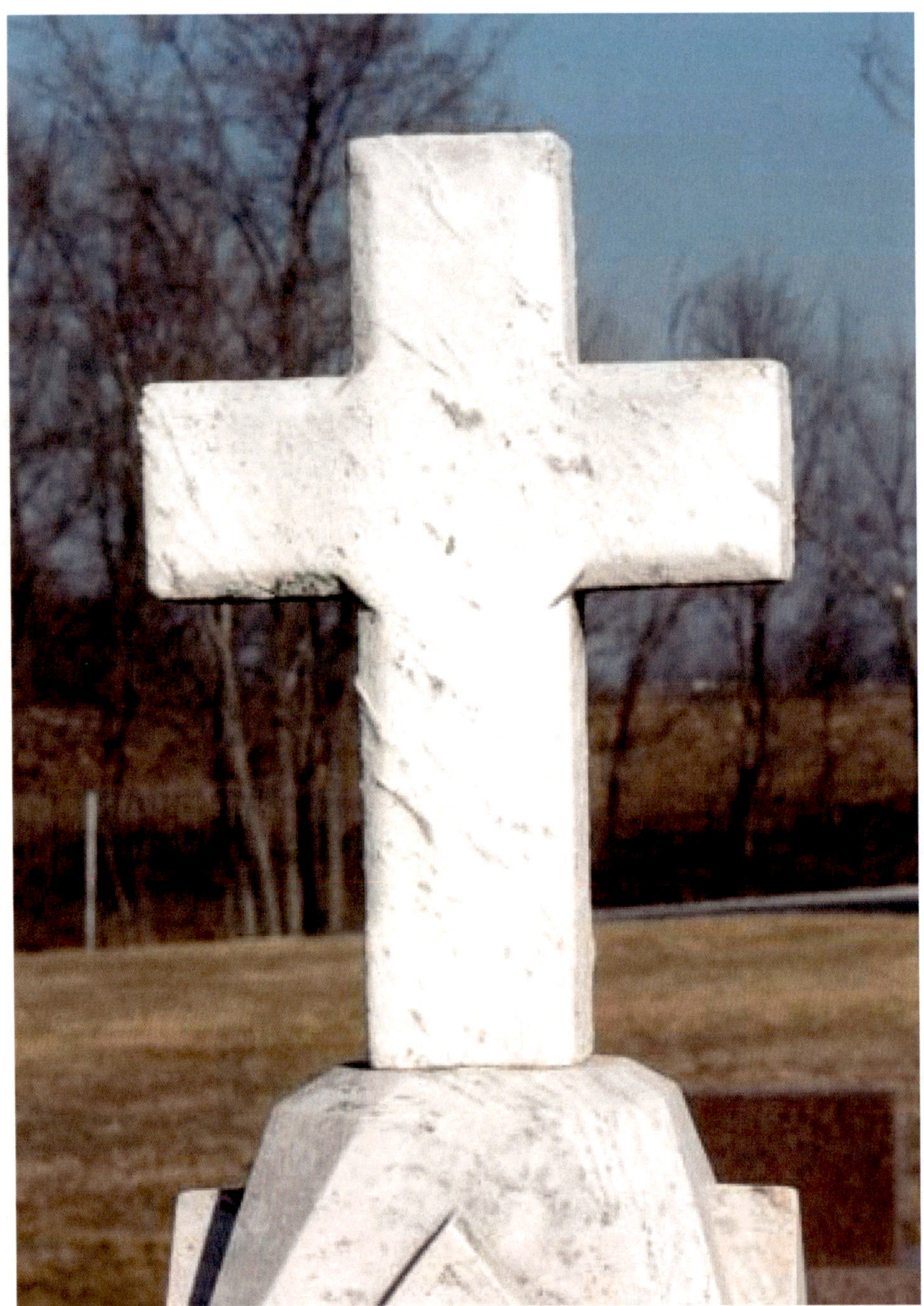

CROSSES

Although today the cross is usually recognized as a Christian symbol, it actually pre-dates Christianity by many centuries. A cross is a very simple geometric design and is easy to create. Even something as casual as sticks falling accidentally may form such a pattern. As a design, the cross was commonly used for decoration, and in some cultures it had symbolic and religious meanings as well. The ancient Assyrians, Egyptians, Greeks, Hindus, and Mayans, among other cultures, used cross designs rendered on stone, on pottery, and in metal.

"Cross" derives from the Latin *crux*. In Middle English the word was *cros*, although sometimes the word *rood* was used interchangeably. Old Norse *kross*, Danish and Swedish *kors*, and Welsh *croes* all mean substantially the same thing. Immigrants from all of the above areas are numerous in Iowa and in the Midwest.

The word "cross" refers to two lines which intersect at right angles. The rood originally was defined as a pole, but in common usage it became the rood cross, representing the instrument of Jesus's crucifixion.

Interpretations vary about exactly what Jesus was crucified on. Whether the martyrdom was on a tree, a stake, or an actual cross, the cross design is widely accepted as a symbol throughout the world. The historical accuracy of any belief is not at issue.

The number of different cross designs is extensive and not all types have formal names. These many forms of crosses are common throughout recorded history, and this universality makes it one of the most common of all symbols. Certainly the cross is the most pervasive symbol used on the grave markers of Christians. Although its use fell out of favor with some Protestant denominations from the 16th century to the early 19th century, its use has again become common in Iowa and across the United States. Although crosses of various designs are more common in Roman Catholic cemeteries than in others, they also are found on the grave markers of many other Christian denominations.

The following list includes types of crosses ordinarily used as grave markers or as symbolic ornamentation on grave markers in Iowa and in the United States. Because of the association of the cross with Christianity, and because virtually all of the grave markers which are discussed in this study mark the graves of Christians, there will be minimal attention to the uses of the cross as a non-Christian symbol, unless it is necessary to understand the roots of some designs.

THE ANCHOR CROSS

(see "Anchor," page 17)

There are at least ten possible anchor cross designs, but all of them have one similarity. The vertical bar of the anchor has a crossbar at the top, which renders the figure cross-like in appearance. It is unlikely that the use of an anchor cross on a grave marker indicates that the deceased had a connection with the sea or with the navy. When that is intended, other symbols are more likely to be used. Almost always the anchor cross is used to indicate the soul or life-saving use of an anchor. Thus it is a symbol of hope.

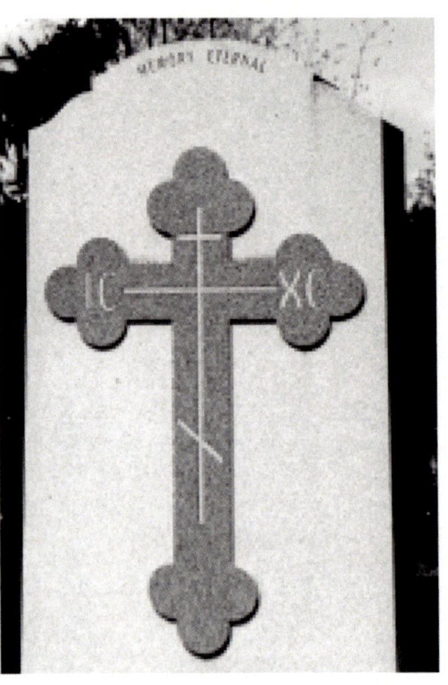

THE BOTONEE CROSS

This type of cross is sometimes called the "budded cross," because of the three lobes on each end of the arms. The three lobes represent the Trinity. When a three-dimensional cross form is used as a grave marker, the Botonee cross design is one of the shapes commonly used. It is not as common as the Latin cross. A familiar use of the Botonee cross is its appearance on the top of church steeples. This design is recognizable as an additional embellishment of the Latin cross. Mostly the Botonee cross is used for grave markers made of metal.

THE CELTIC CROSS

Many grave markers in Iowa and in the United States are in the form of Celtic crosses. This is the common name for an ornamented and stylized cross usually related to Ireland. Actually Celtic crosses can be found throughout the British Isles and in all areas where people from the British Isles settled.

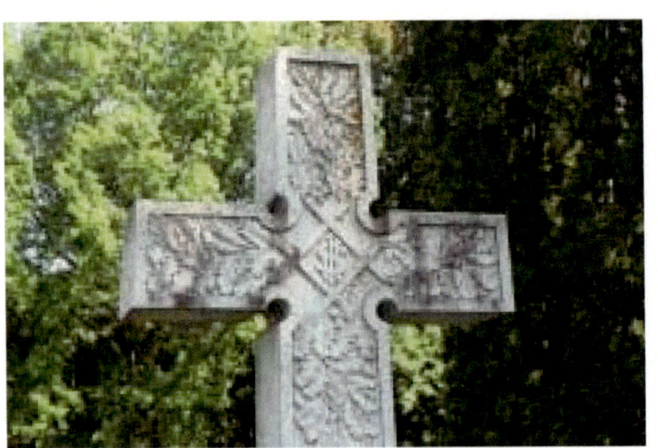

There is some confusion about the origin of this design. When seen in the British Isles such a cross may be a high cross, a market cross, a war memorial cross, or the marker on a grave. High crosses were erected to mark sacred and other public spaces. These spaces became the focal points for gatherings and celebrations for Christians and others. High crosses also were used to mark the boundaries between parishes. In the British Isles, almost all Celtic crosses were erected prior to the 12th century CE.

Commonly the panel and arms of Celtic crosses in Ireland were carved with biblical scenes and stories, and they were used for religious instruction. This was useful when the population was largely illiterate. These biblical scenes and Celtic symbols are examples of great stone carving skills.

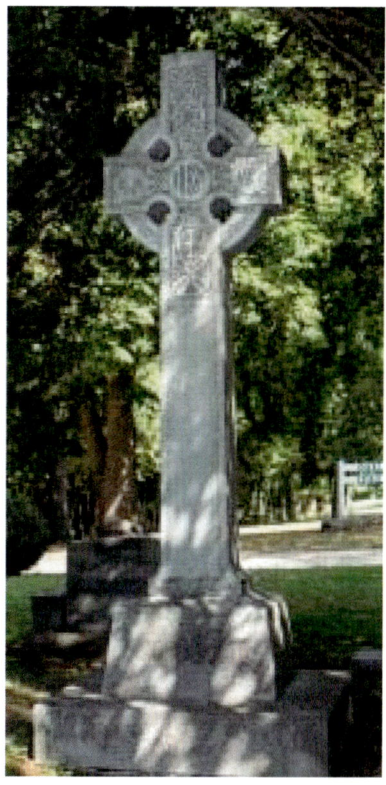

In the United States it was not until after the middle of the 19th century that Celtic crosses came to be used as grave markers. Partially this was due to immigration from Ireland, and partially it was a style that became popular because of its inherent beauty. In Iowa and the rest of the United States, Celtic crosses used as grave markers are likely to be carved with designs that are ornamental, rather than religious. The Celtic knot is the most common design. Of course this has a pagan religious interpretation, but it is unlikely that the persons choosing such a grave marker were aware of these meanings. In Iowa there are many grave markers in the form of stylized Celtic crosses, whether they mark the graves of people of British descent or not.

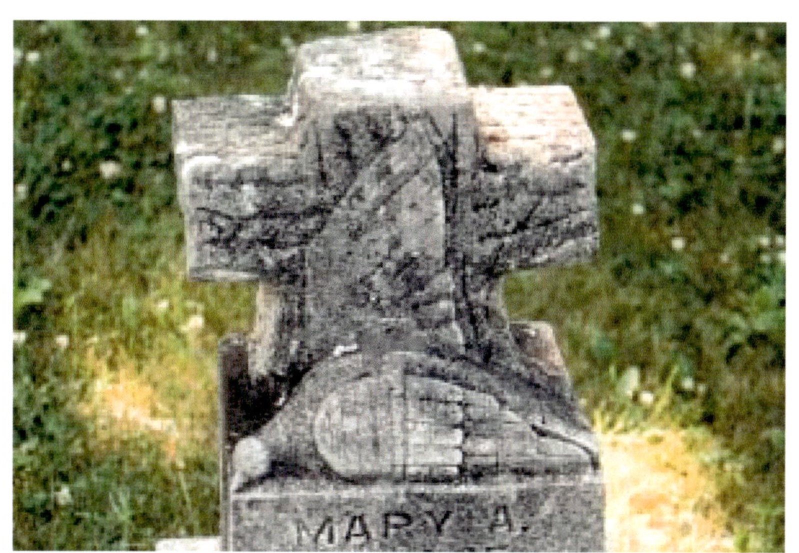

THE GREEK CROSS

On a Greek cross, all four arms are uniform in length and shape. Early examples of this design have been found on grave markers in the catacombs of Rome. By the 10th century CE, this design was used as the official banner of Genoa, and the same design was carried by the Crusaders from England. In England this form of cross is known as the Cross of St. George and forms part of the Union Jack, the official flag of the United Kingdom. When rendered in red on a white background, this cross is the international symbol of the Red Cross. Rarely is this cross design used as a full grave marker by itself, but is more commonly used on the face of stone grave markers as a Christian symbol.

THE LATIN CROSS

By far the most common cross design used for grave markers in Iowa and the United States is the Latin cross. The Latin cross has its origin in the western branch of Christianity, the Church of Rome. On a Latin cross, the vertical member is longer than the horizontal member, which is inserted at a right angle. When the corpus figure is added, the cross becomes a crucifix. The technical terms for the members of the Latin cross are *stipe* for the vertical member and *patibulum* for the cross arm member.

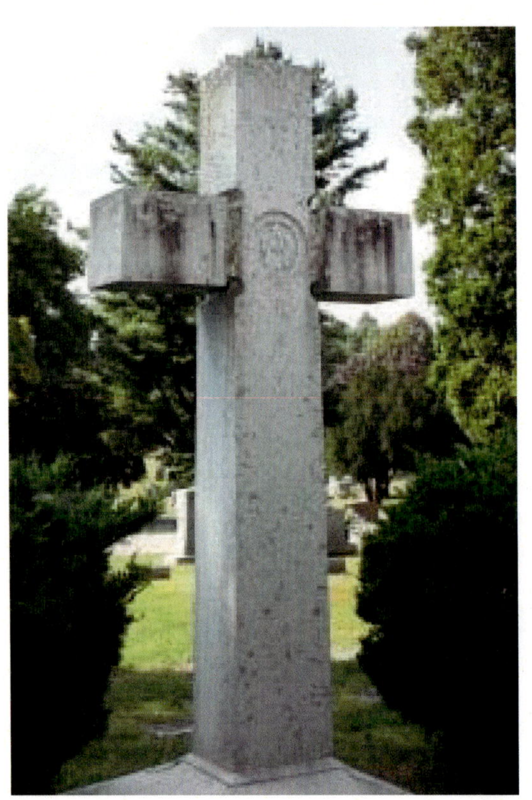

Roman Catholic cemeteries are prone to having a majority of the grave markers of this design, both in Iowa and throughout the United States. In Roman Catholic cemeteries, the Latin cross frequently is found in three-dimensional form as a grave marker. It also is common as a design on the face of other shapes of stone grave markers.

In Christianity the Latin cross is known as *crux ordinaire*. As a Christian symbol, it replaced earlier symbols such as the fish, the lamb, the anchor, and other designs, though the earlier designs remain in use as symbolic embellishment on the face of stone grave markers. Sometimes the letters IHS are found at the intersection of the arms of the Latin cross. This is an abbreviation for the name of Jesus.

Though the Latin cross is closely associated with Christianity, similar designs have been found in much earlier times and in places as distant as China, Africa, and in Bronze Age Scandinavia. There are theories that in the periods before Christianity, the symbol in northern Europe may have meant the hammer of Thor, god of thunder and lightning.

Another theory about the origin of this type of cross is that it was the symbol of the earth. The arms of the cross point to the cardinal compass points. Perhaps the cross represented the elements of earth, water, air, and fire.

In some ways the Latin cross resembles the human form with arms outstretched. This same form is often used as the floor plan for Christian churches and cathedrals. It is known as the cruciform floor plan.

THE ORTHODOX CROSS

The Orthodox cross is a variation of other Christian cross designs. It is common throughout Eastern Orthodox Churches such as Greek Orthodox, Russian Orthodox, and others. Its roots are in the Byzantine church at Constantinople, which never accepted the jurisdiction of the Church of Rome. The Orthodox cross has three horizontal cross bars on a vertical member. The top cross bar is shorter in length than the middle bar, which resembles the Latin Cross. The lower cross bar is fixed at a slant, which has different meanings in different traditions.

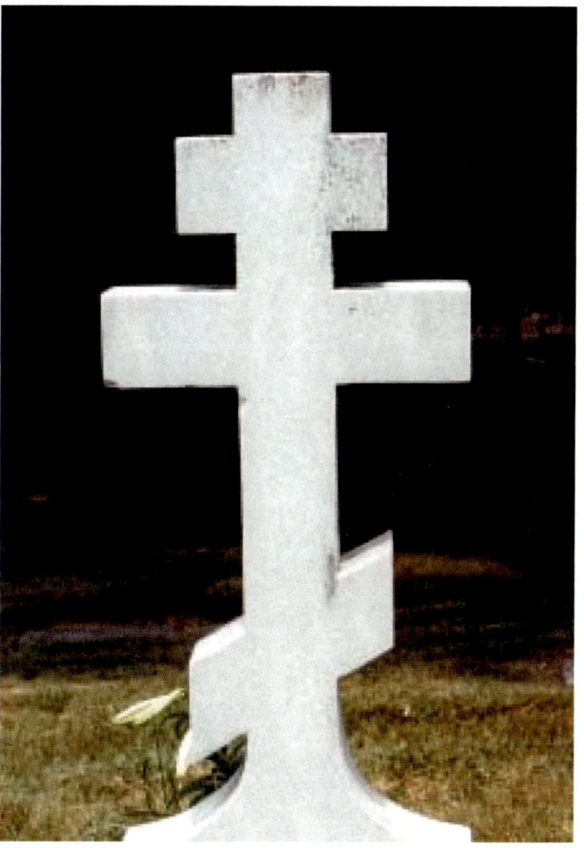

The top cross bar of the Orthodox cross often bears the acronym INRI, the Christian abbreviation for "Jesus of Nazareth, King of the Jews." This expression is called *titulus*. The middle bar rarely has any additional carving on it. The lower, slanted bar, according to some traditions, is an indication that at the day of the last judgment, those on Christ's right hand will ascend to heaven. This tradition is based on the story about the two men on either side of Jesus at the time of crucifixion, one of whom was saved while the other was not.

There are numerous examples of Orthodox Crosses used as grave markers in Iowa and in the United States. It indicates membership in an orthodox church.

THE POMMEE CROSS

The Pommee cross is similar to the Botonee cross, except that it has only a single lobe at the end of each arm instead of the trinity symbol. Originally this cross was known as the Bezant cross. It was renamed because of the resemblance of the lobes at the end to apples, hence the name Pommee. There is an unverified theory that the Pommee cross was designed to represent the fruits of a good Christian life.

The Pommee cross is sometimes used as the design for three-dimensional grave markers, most often made of metal, and it also is used as an emblem on the steeples of Christian churches. There are many examples of the Pommee cross in Iowa and in the United States.

THE SALTIRE CROSS

The Saltire cross also is known as the Cross of St. Andrew. The arms of this cross form a diagonal, resembling the letter X. This design appears repeatedly on the coinage of early Christian emperors of Rome. By the 10th century CE, the design was adopted by the Eastern branch of the Christian church as a symbol of its power.

The most common use of the Saltire cross is in the flag of Scotland, which – combined with the Cross of St. George – forms the Union Jack, the flag of the United Kingdom. While the Saltire cross is sometimes used as a symbol on the face of stone grave markers, its shape makes it unwieldy for use in a 3-dimensional form. Examples of the Saltire Cross are rare in Iowa, and not common in the United States.

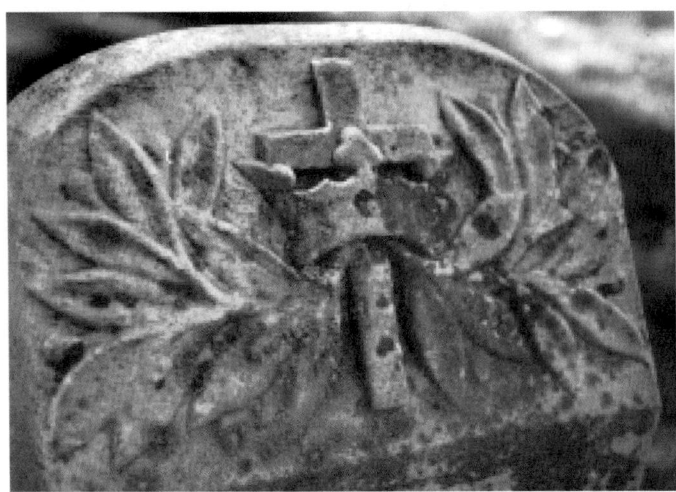

SUMMARY

Most of the several dozen cross designs are variations on the simpler Latin cross or Greek cross. Very rarely are any of the other designs used for grave markers, although some of them might appear as ornamentation on grave markers. Those used for such ornamentation might or might not have any symbolic significance. The major exceptions to the use of the Latin cross or the Greek cross for grave markers include the Celtic cross and the Orthodox cross. Both of these are elaborations on the Latin cross. There are occasions when the Anchor cross appears to be an independent symbol rather than a variation. In almost every case, alterations, embellishments, or additions do not erase the basic design. They only enhance it.

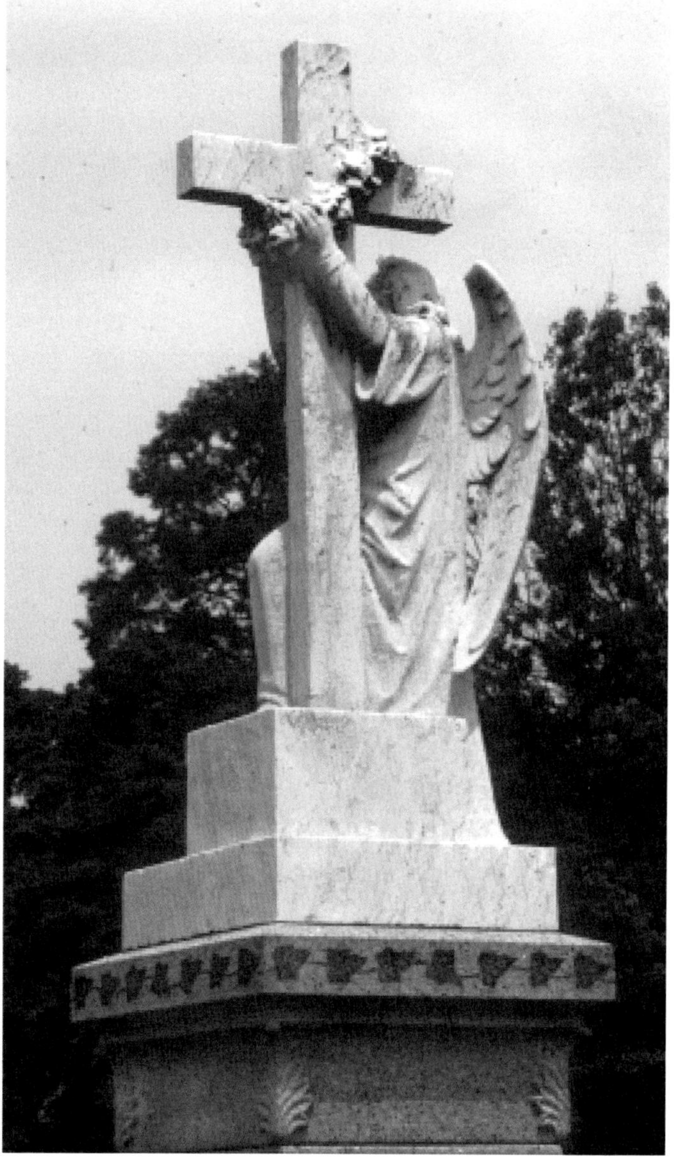

Since the cross is one of the most basic symbols in Christianity, it is not surprising that for centuries people have used the cross design in churches and on grave markers. It is rare to visit a cemetery and not find multiple uses of the cross design, as three-dimensional markers and as ornamentation on the faces of markers of different shapes and made of different materials. While the cross seems to be most prevalent in Roman Catholic cemeteries, it also is very common in cemeteries controlled by other liturgical churches, such as Episcopal and Lutheran. And it is commonly used to mark graves in United States military cemeteries.

Interestingly, though the cross is now a basic symbol of Christianity, it did not come into general use until about three centuries after the crucifixion of Christ. Not until the reign of the Emperor Constantine did the cross become the principal symbol of the Christian Church. From that time on, it gradually replaced earlier symbols - the fish, the lamb, the anchor, etc.

MILITARY GRAVE MARKER SYMBOLS

Among the several symbols with a military connotation are the eagle, the flag, the sword, and the shield. During the 19th century, such military symbols were almost always connected with military service, which was limited to men. Soldiers who had served on active duty, perhaps in combat, were proud to be remembered with these military symbols. It mattered not at all whether they were killed in action or whether they were veterans honored after having served in the military.

The United States government has been issuing grave markers for military veterans for well over a century. The designs of the headstones have changed over time,

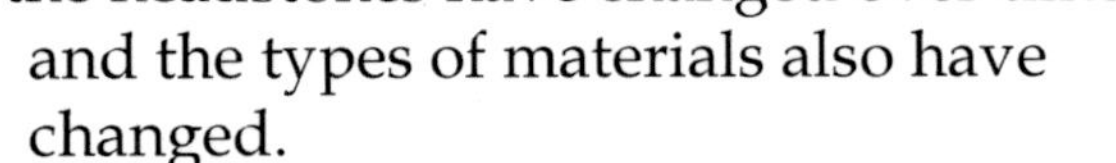

and the types of materials also have changed.

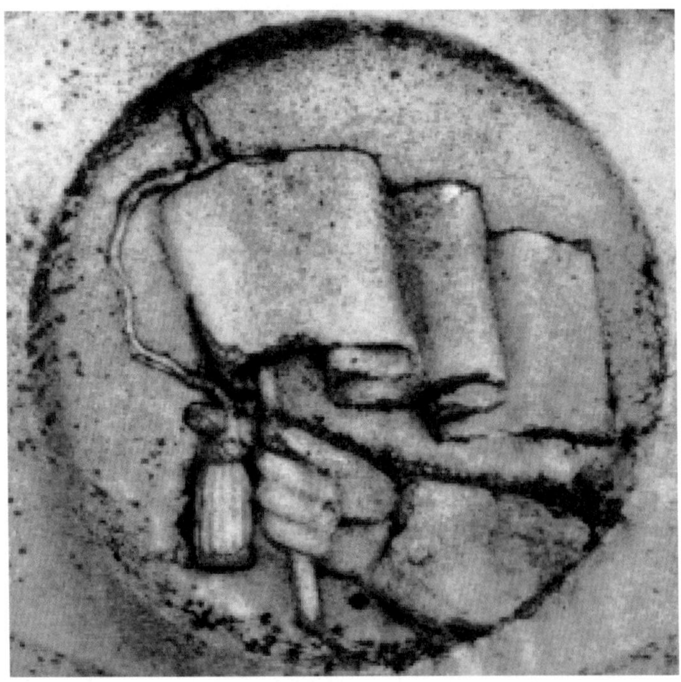

Some of the designs included symbols, but for the most part early military headstones were simply identification markers. The first headstones issued in 1873 included name, rank, unit, and war service of the veteran whose burial place they marked. These markers often did not include birth or death dates. The headstones were erected in National Cemeteries only, and at first were intended only for Civil War service. Later they were used for the veterans of the Revolutionary War, the War of 1812, the Mexican War, and all Indian campaigns. The first headstones were made of marble or other durable stone.

The latest change of federal government policy was in 2001. Since that time, government-issue grave markers may be made of marble, granite, or bronze. They may be upright or flat, be used in a niche, or may be a medallion which can be affixed to an existing, privately-purchased headstone. They may be placed in any private or public cemetery.

When a military headstone has been damaged by weather, vandalism, accident, or any other cause, a replacement headstone can be furnished.

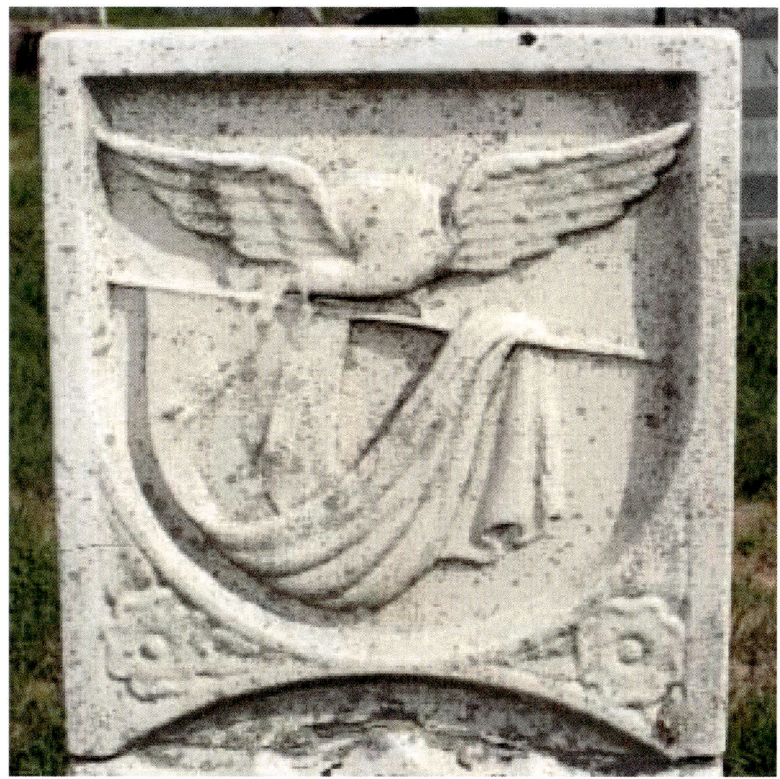

EAGLE

An eagle on any grave marker most often served as both a military and a patriotic symbol. Eagles appeared frequently in association with other military or patriotic symbols, seldom being the only symbol on a headstone. From 1873 until the death of the last Civil War veteran, the eagle seems to have been the symbol of choice for men who were members of the Grand Army of the Republic (G.A.R.), the veterans' organization formed after the War Between the States.

Because women serve in the military and in combat during the 21st century, perhaps the date of death will allow a different insight into the meaning of the eagle as a symbol.

Eagles used as symbols on grave markers appear in various forms and positions. Most representations show eagles with outstretched wings. Sometimes the eagle is at rest with wings at the sides. Very occasionally, only the eagle's head is used as a symbol. In any of these cases the eagle was intended to represent courage and bravery.

FLAG

Not only are flags common symbols on grave markers, actual flags are common in cemeteries during such commemorations as Decoration Day (Memorial Day) and Armistice Day (Veterans Day). The avenues of flags encountered on those days mostly consist of flags which have been used to drape the caskets of veterans during their funerals. It has become the custom in many cemeteries to place small flags near the headstones of all graves of veterans during those same commemorations.

The flag is the symbol of honor and patriotism. It should be noted that with very few exceptions, flags carved on the face of headstones are not true representations of the United States flag at the time of burial. Because of the difficulties of delicate carving or etching on stone, few flags on grave markers are accurate as to the numbers of stars and stripes portrayed. This does not lessen the power of the symbol. Since the use of laser etching has become common, the accuracy of numbers of stars and stripes can be much more precise.

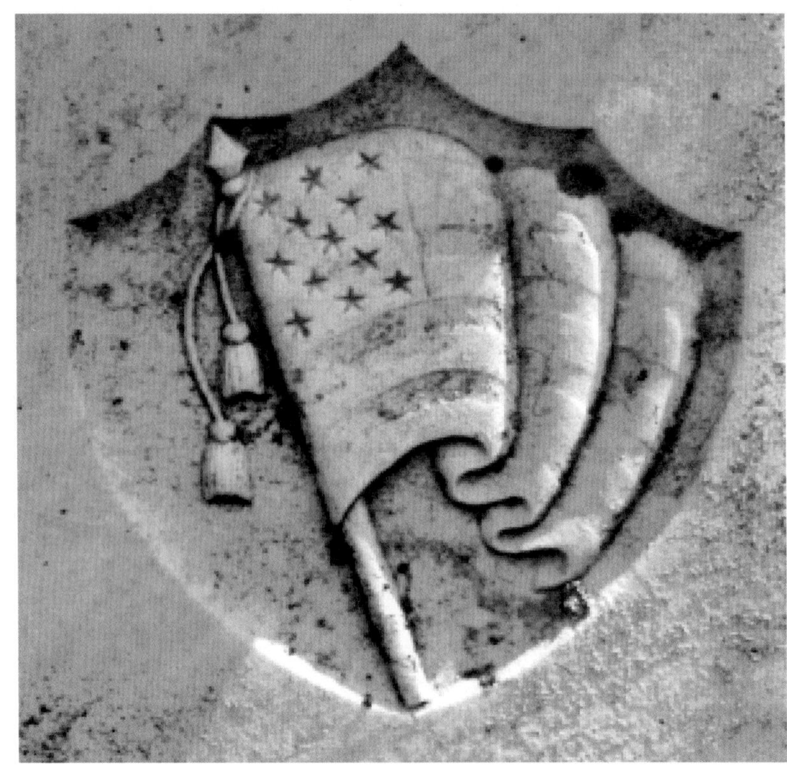

Flags used on veterans' graves in the 19th and early 20th centuries were exclusively for men, if the headstone was issued by the federal government. In the 21st century the symbol may be on the graves of women veterans. Of course it was always possible to use any of the military symbols on anyone's grave marker, if the marker was privately purchased.

SWORD

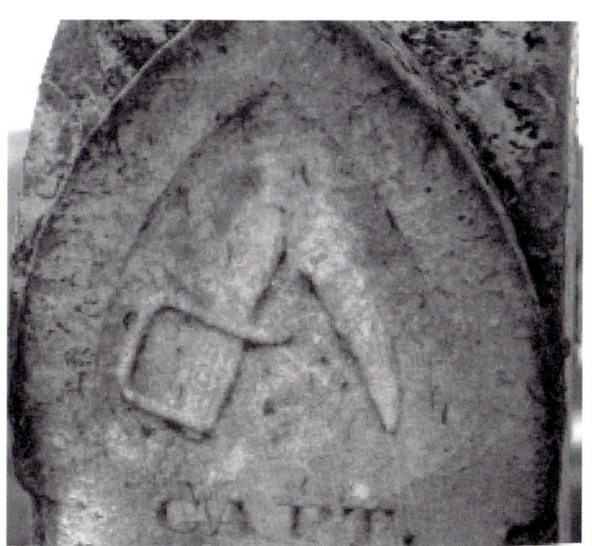

Almost certainly the sword has always been associated with military service of some sort. This would have been true in Europe during the medieval period. In most circumstances it was always true in Iowa and the entire United States. Swords are emblems of courage, bravery, and skill. Swords were typically not issued to all personnel in a military unit at any time, so there was an element of higher honor with their use because of the higher rank of the person whose burial they mark.

The sword seldom appears on a grave marker without an association with some other symbol.

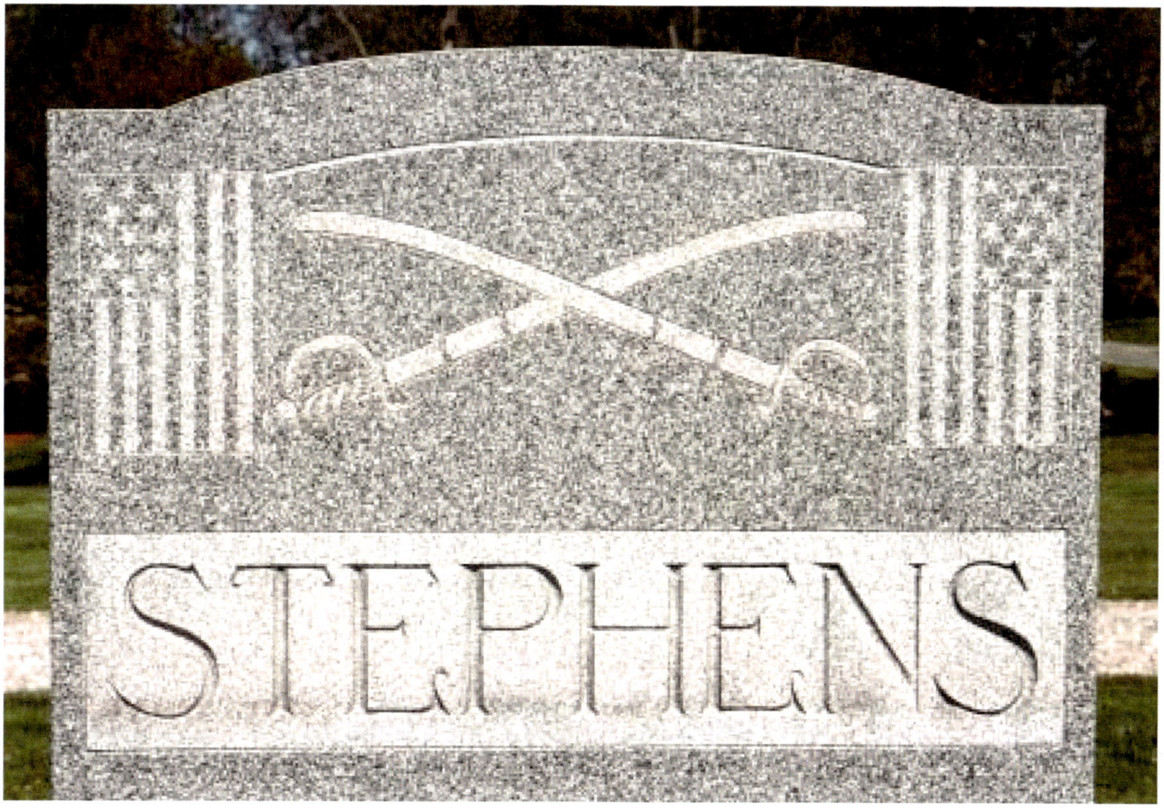

SHIELD

The shield was a symbol of courage and bravery.

An outline of a shield became a regular feature of several different designs for grave markers issued by the United States government. In 1873 Secretary of War William Worth Belknap of Keokuk, Iowa authorized the first design for military headstones. Those markers were 4 inches thick, 10 inches wide, and had to have at least 12 inches of height extending above the surface of the ground. The design incorporated a sunken shield pattern, in which the inscription appeared in relief carving.

In some instances, more recent replacement headstones may have a raised shield pattern on the surface.

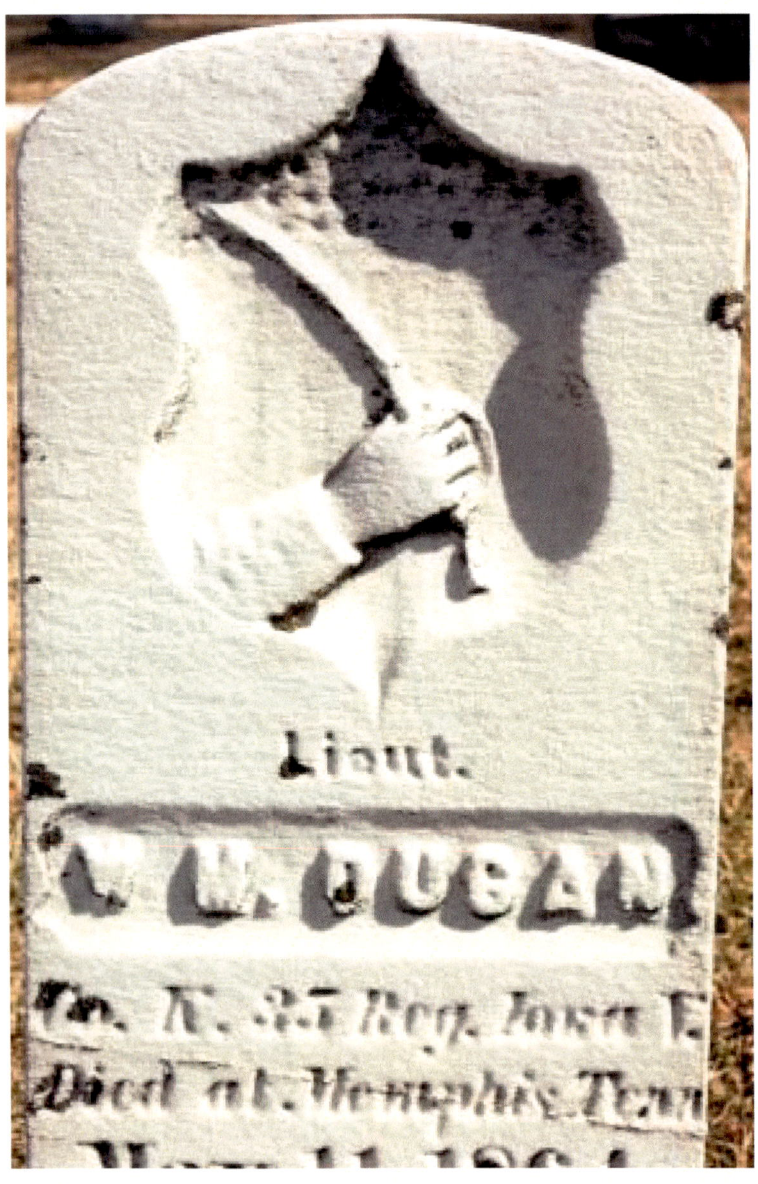

SYMBOLS NOT OFTEN USED IN THE MIDWEST

Several symbols are closely related to death but are seldom used on grave markers in Iowa or in the Midwest. Because some of them do appear occasionally on grave markers in Iowa, it is proper to consider their several meanings.

The symbols are: skeleton; skeleton and scythe or sickle; skeleton with hour glass; death's head; winged death's head; skull and crossed bones (usually written crossbones); hour glass; winged hour glass; and willow and urn.

Each of these symbols was common in Medieval Europe, and some were known as well in other parts of the world in ancient times. On occasion they may appear singly, but often they occur together in a variety of multiples. They are not always in the same relationships with each other.

In medieval artistic renderings, some or all of these symbols appear in what was called the *dans macabre*, or "the dance of death."

The skeleton, with or without a scythe, sickle, or hour glass, was the most common symbol of death during the Middle Ages in Europe, and it was brought to North America by the English immigrants.

All of these symbols have been used in the United States, but the most common symbol in this country tended to be the skull and crossbones and the hour glass. Both symbols were relatively common in the grave yards of Puritan New England in the 17th and 18th centuries.

Even more common in that area was the innovation known as the death's head, which might be carved with or without wings on a grave marker. The Puritan religious leaders frowned on the idea of ornamenting grave markers, but they were willing to allow all of the above symbols because of their instructional value. A winged death's head, which gradually became more common, was simply a skull with stylized wings emerging on either side of the head. The skull and crossbones also was a very common symbol on Puritan grave markers throughout the 17th and 18th centuries. Numerous studies have verified that these two designs are the prevalent symbols in New England.

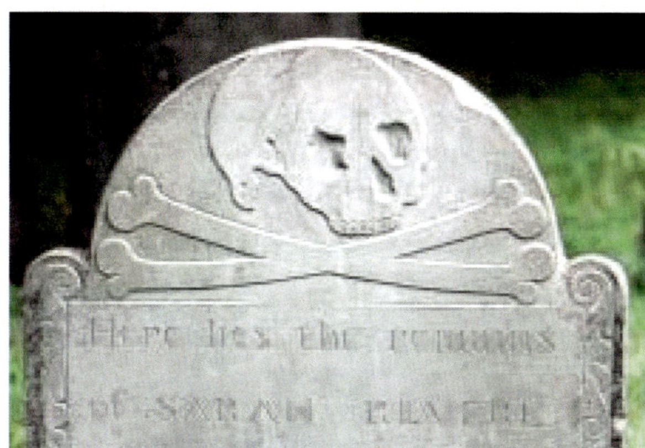

The skull and crossbones symbol reminds most people in the United States of the flag sometimes supposedly used by pirates, known as the "Jolly Roger." Reportedly the first use of such a flag was by Emanuel Wynne in 1715. The French pirate flew a flag that had a white skull and

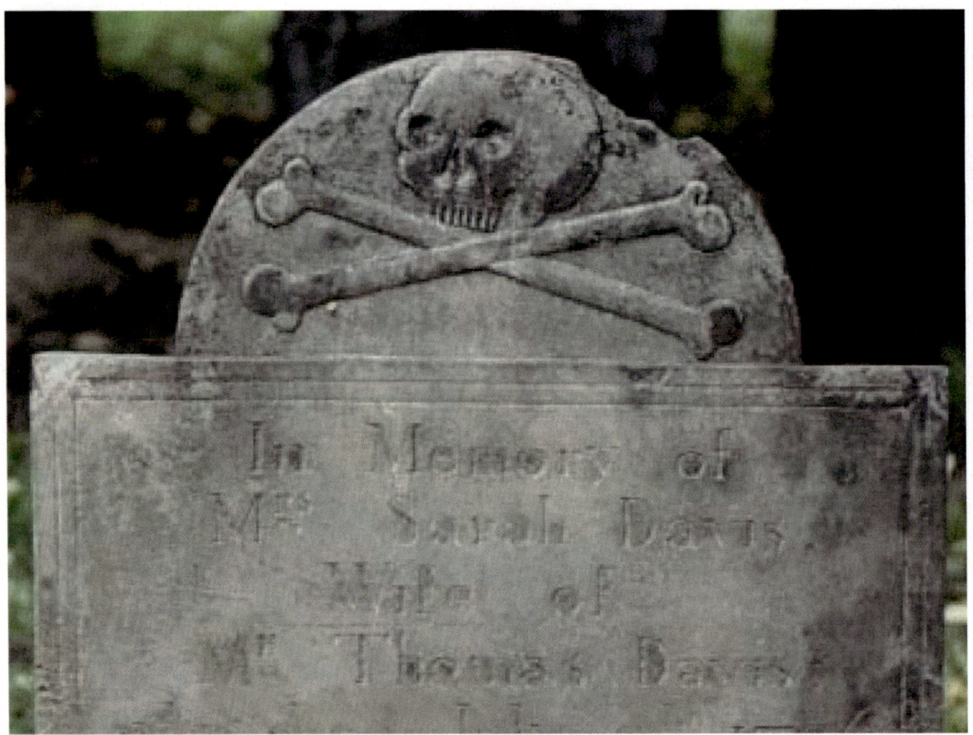

crossbones on a black background, with an hour glass beneath it. This same skull and crossbones symbol also was used by the Knights Templar during the Crusades to reclaim the Holy Land from the Muslims. Later it seems to have been utilized in one or more of the degrees of the Masonic Order.

On a grave marker in Iowa or anywhere in the United States, both the skeleton and the skull and crossbones simply are symbols of death. Quite often in Puritan New England they were used as a lesson or a warning, while in the Midwest they were more likely used as simply another death symbol. In Iowa and the Midwest these symbols most often appear on monuments made of white bronze. Both symbols were among the many castings of symbols offered by white bronze foundries. It is rare to find a skeleton without a scythe or sickle in any United States cemetery.

Sometimes a skeleton symbol is portrayed holding an hour glass and a scythe/ sickle, and sometimes only one or the other object. If a skeleton holds both a scythe/ sickle and an hour glass, it is more or less a triple symbol of death. Since all three symbols represent death, it is well to note the nuances involved.

A scythe is a normal instrument used in agriculture and is needed for harvesting or reaping the grain. Thus the symbol came to be nicknamed "the grim reaper." A skeleton, especially when hooded, sometimes was known as "Father Time." When used on a grave marker this probably indicated that the person buried in the grave had reached or exceeded the biblical span of three score and ten years. In a symbolic sense that person was ripe and ready for harvest. People saw the relationship between harvesting grain, and harvesting souls. (Psalm 90:10)

The scythe is similar to the later, and much more common, symbol of the sickle and sheaf of wheat. The latter symbol also carries out the connection with agriculture. The sickle and sheaf of wheat are more often found in Iowa and the Midwest than are the skeleton and scythe.

The hour glass is one of the symbols representing the passage of time. People in the 17th and 18th centuries would have readily recognized the connection with *Memento Mori*. The hour glass meant the sands of time and the years of life gradually were passing. But if the hour glass was reversed, then it symbolized restoration, becoming the promise of a renewal of life in another form.

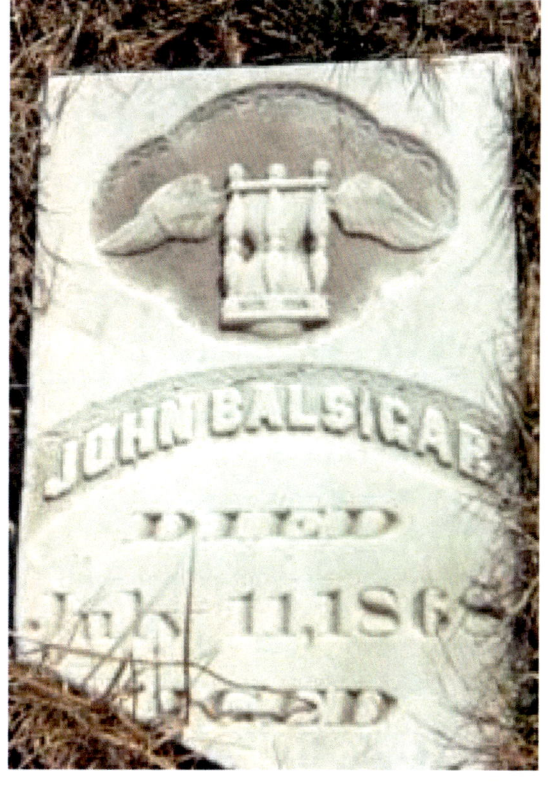

In any case, the hour glass was an indication of unstoppable movement, a finality that no human power could halt. A winged hour glass is a sort of double death symbol. The sands of time not only are passing, they are flying by. The hour glass symbol, with or without wings, is to be found in some Iowa and Midwest cemeteries.

The willow and urn was a common 18th-century symbol throughout the English colonies in North America. Not only was it often found on grave markers, it was just as common on artworks, textiles (particularly samplers), and other surfaces of interior decoration.

While the weeping willow was a symbol of death, it was more readily recognized as an expression of grief and mourning. Sometimes the willow shades an urn. Sometimes the willow shades a monument. And frequently the symbol is enhanced by the presence of a grieving female figure. There are few known examples of this symbol in Iowa cemeteries.

The skeleton was an emblem of Saturn in the ancient world, signifying the impermanence of life, indicating a natural cycle in which all life will end. End of life in this form simply was to allow renewal of life in another form. Saturn was the Roman god of time. The equivalent Greek god of time was Cronos, also spelled Chronos or Kronos. Cronos was associated with the scythe, the sickle, and the hour glass.

Both the Greek and Roman civilizations believed in the connection between the sickle and the crescent moon. The sickle represented the inexorable flow of time, both destructive and constructive. Time was the devourer of all things, but vitality could be renewed. The crescent moon was a symbol of finality, but also the harbinger of a new birth.

Crops are cut down at harvest, but they are reborn during the next growing season. In its simplest terms, a skeleton represents mortality and death. Whether the figure is hooded or not is irrelevant. Also irrelevant is whether the skeleton figure is holding additional symbols of death, such as the scythe, the sickle, or the hour glass.

The most common representation was of a skeleton holding a scythe or sickle. Sometimes the skeleton is hooded. Sometimes the skeleton is holding an hour glass. In any of these cases the symbol presents the idea that death is inevitable, that death ultimately comes to every person.

Therefore, the people of that time thought that it was desirable and appropriate for each person to prepare for his or her own death. A variety of epitaphs show this same idea.

One of the most famous epitaphs appears numerous times and in numerous forms:

Remember friends, as you pass by,
As you are now, so once was I,
As I am now, so you must be,
Prepare for death and follow me.

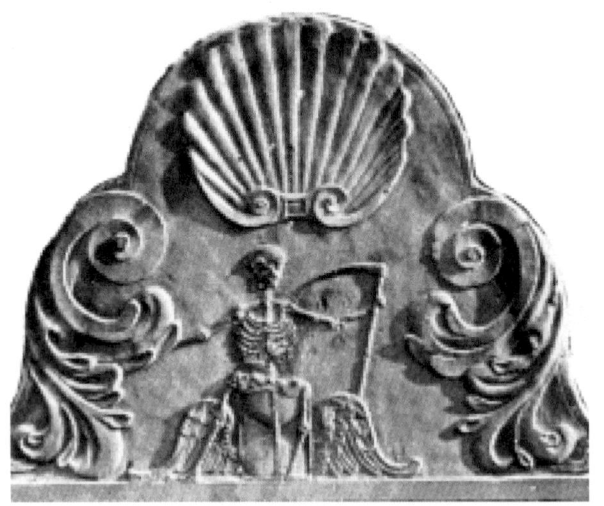

There are at least fourteen different versions of this same verse. Its origin is shrouded in the mysteries of time. Some references state that it was first found on a Roman military officer's grave stone. Other sources believe that it was derived from one of the Odes of Horace, the great Roman poet. We know that it was used in Europe as early as 1376, when it was carved on the tomb of Edward, the Black Prince, in Canterbury Cathedral. That particular version, translated from the Norman French to English, is:

Whoso thou be that passeth by;
Where these corps entombed lie:
Understand what I shall say,
At this time speak I may,
Such as thou art, sometimes was I,
Such as I am, such shalt thou be.

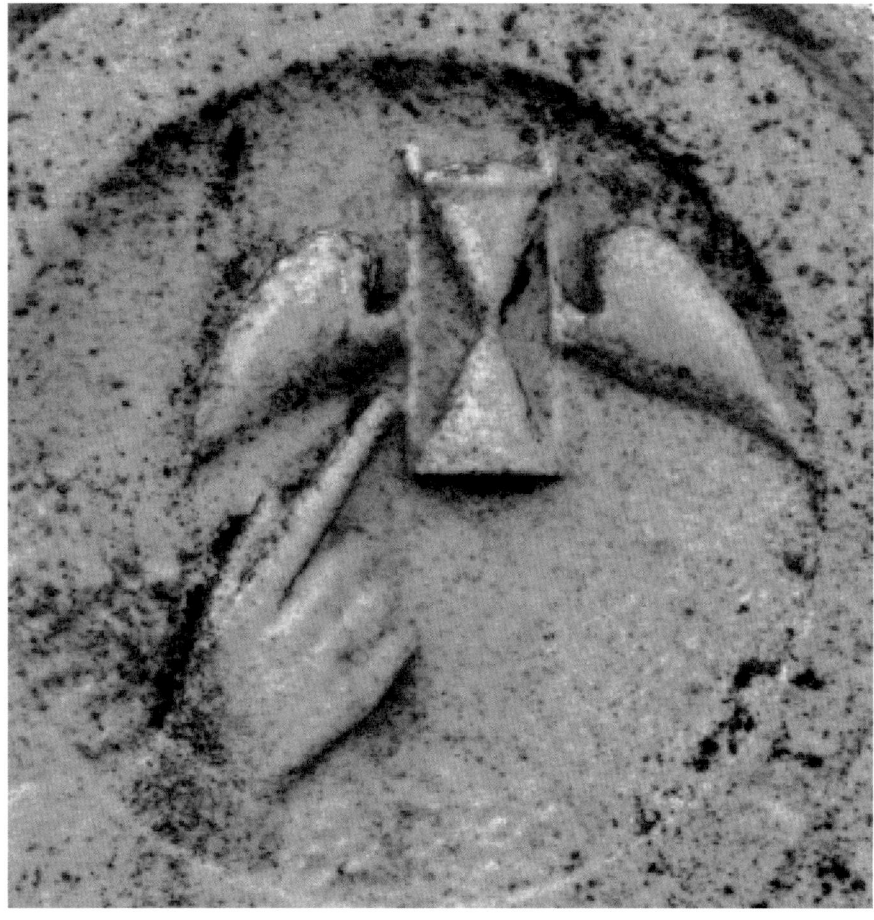

Another version has been found on a tomb in Perthshire, Scotland, dated 1666:

As ye ar nou
So onc was ay
As ay am so sal
Ye be remembre
Man that thou
Mist dei

The Latin expression, from whatever original source, is as follows: *Fui quod es, eris quod sum.* This has been translated as: "I once was what you are, you will be what I am."

During the Medieval period in Europe, there were guide books to help people prepare for what was referred to as a "good death." The Latin phrase *Memento Mori* was the expression most often used. It usually was translated as "Remember, you must die."

Other Latin expressions also came into common usage. *Tempus fugit* meant "Time flies." *Hora fugit* meant "The hour flees." All of these expressions are closely related to *ars moriendi*, "the art of dying."

Following the directions found in such guide books was supposed to lead the reader to a "good death." Of course all of these ideas stemmed from a religious teaching which urged the contemplation of the transitory nature of earthly life and possessions.

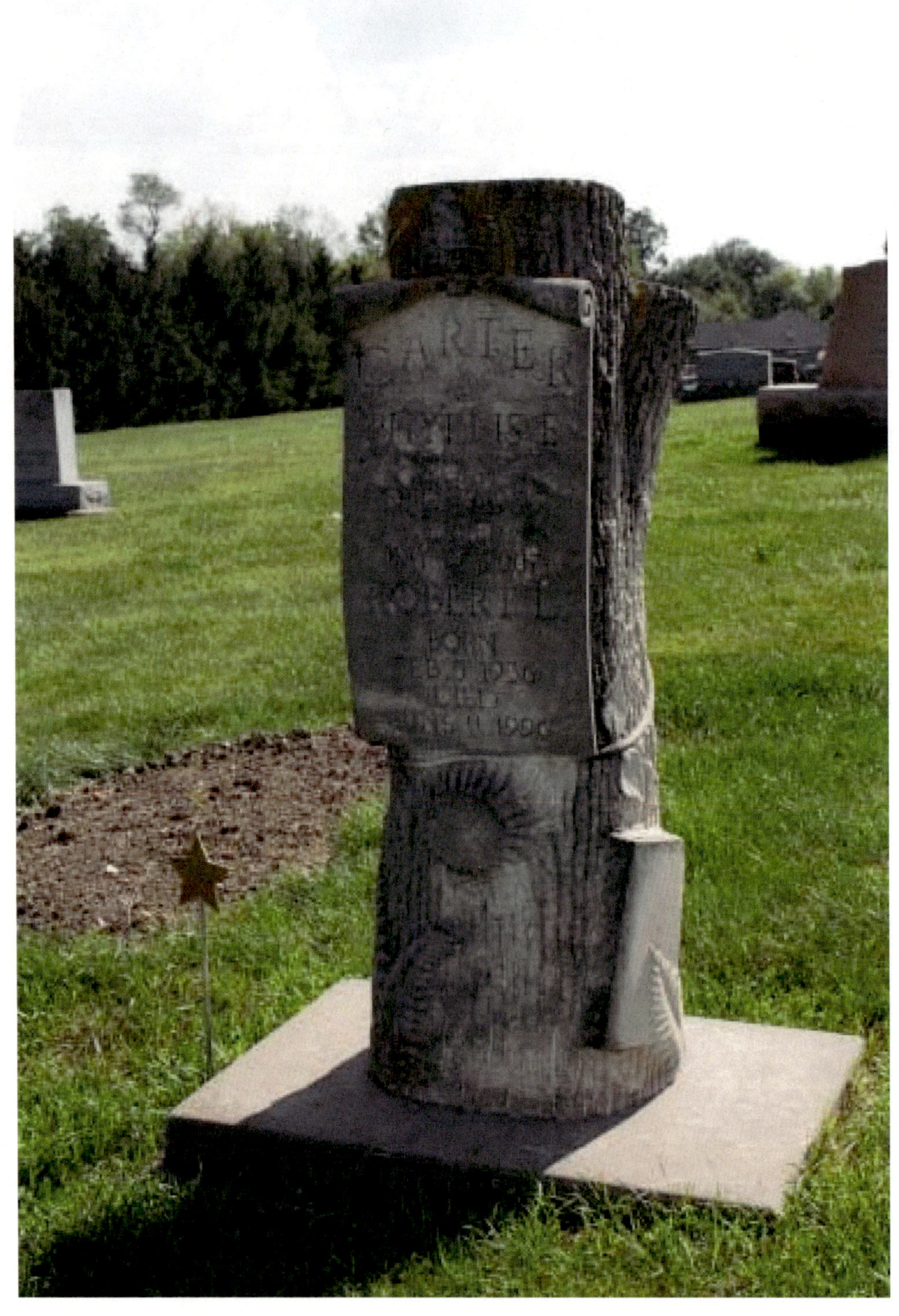
CARTER

STONE USED FOR GRAVE MARKERS

The majority of grave markers in the United States are made of stone. Until the past two centuries it was most convenient to use readily-available local deposits of stone. Not until the 19th century was it usual to bring into an area varieties of stone not found in the immediate vicinity or within the adjacent region. If stone to be converted into grave markers had to be brought from a distance, it was more expensive than local stone. Therefore imported stone was less available to the ordinary person. People who wished to demonstrate conspicuous expenditure seemed to prefer stone brought in from a distance. Because this practice cost more, it led to the attitude among some people that the imported stone was better. Prevailing fashion and popularity meant that stone brought from a distance came to be the material of choice for many grave markers.

Monument dealers quickly recognized and took advantage of the opportunity. Sometimes dealers labeled their establishments "Marble Yards," even though the grave markers that they sold actually were made of limestone or granite.

Certain types of stone have been used more commonly for grave markers than other kinds of stone. Sometimes this use is because of local or regional availability. In other cases it is because of the ease of shaping and carving. Use may also depend upon what is popular and what is fashionable. There are cases of stone choices being made dependent upon the cost, and on the financial resources of the purchaser.

Without going into complex geological detail, for our purposes stone may be divided into three categories: sedimentary, metamorphic, and igneous.

Grave markers can be and have been made from all three categories of stone, and examples may be found commonly throughout the United States. However, there are some regional patterns as well as groupings based upon technological developments. Some categories of stone are easier than others to carve and to shape with hand tools. Some categories of stone deteriorate more quickly than others, especially when exposed to a climate with a

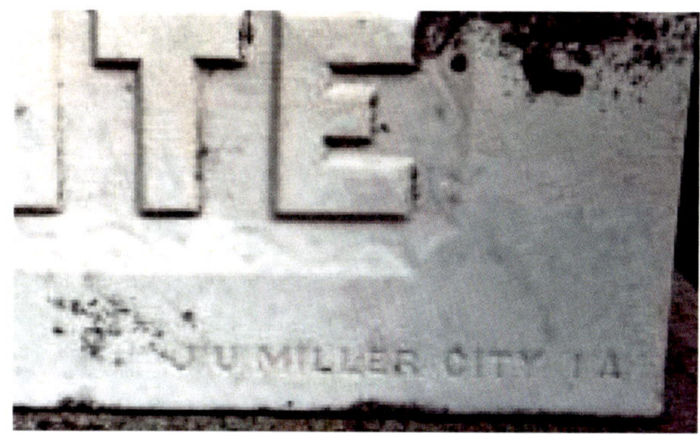

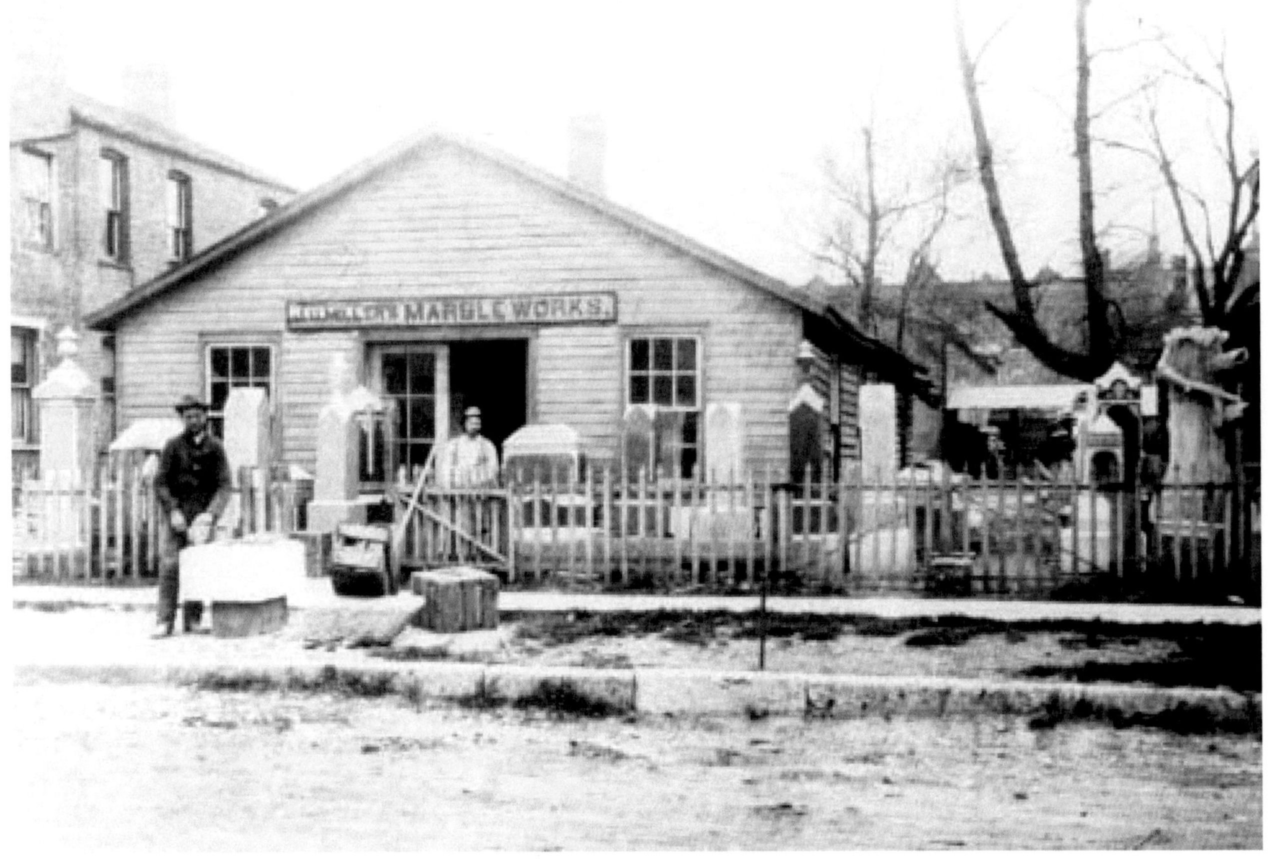

freeze/thaw cycle. The surface of some stone types are more likely to support lichen growth. There are kinds of stone which accommodate the carving of relief lettering and figures, but more kinds of stone which are adaptable to incised and etched lettering and figures.

SEDIMENTARY STONE

This type of stone originated when tiny sedimentary pieces broke off from larger elements, to form rock beds. The pieces then were bonded through millions of years of heat and pressure.

LIMESTONE: Consists mainly of calcite, and ordinarily does not exhibit much graining of crystalline structure. Limestone has a smooth granular surface, and varies in hardness. Common colors are grey, white, black, brown, and yellow. There are limestone quarries in most areas of the United States.

A special type of limestone called "oolitic" is discussed in the glossary. Oolitic

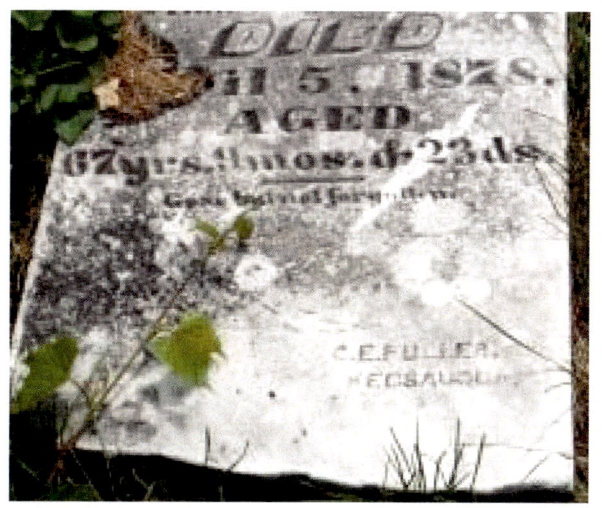

limestone has been used to make grave markers where deposits of the stone were available. It is found most abundantly in the Lawrence County, Indiana region.

Many hundreds of buildings throughout the United States have been constructed of Oolitic limestone from Lawrence County, Indiana. Among the most famous are the Pentagon and the Empire State Building. Oolitic limestone also is famous as the material from which grave markers are made, particularly the tree stump or tree trunk markers favored by members of the Woodmen of the World and the Modern Woodmen of America. These grave markers can be found by the thousands throughout Iowa, the Midwest and the rest of the United States.

SANDSTONE: A very durable formation of sand (quartz grains), usually formed in light brown or reddish colors. It may be bonded by such agents as silica, calcium, clay, or iron oxide. Sandstone was commonly used for grave markers in the 17th and 18th centuries in the Connecticut River valley. It was never a common material for grave markers in Iowa and the Midwest.

SOAPSTONE: This is a very soft stone made of a variety of talc. It is a dense stone that is often resistant to oxidation. There are very few examples of its use for grave markers in Iowa and the Midwest, but it was not uncommon in New England.

METAMORPHIC STONE

This type of stone originates in a natural form through the mixture of heat, pressure, and minerals. The change from one type of rock to another may be a development of a crystalline formation, texture change, or a color change.

MARBLE: This is a re-crystallized limestone that formed when the limestone softened from heat and pressure, and then became marble when a mineral change occurred. The main consistency is calcium and dolomite. Marble occurs in many colors, sometimes is heavily veined, and may show grains. Its hardness rates from 2.5 to 5 on the MOH Scale. Marble is divided into three categories, depending upon the percentage of magnesium carbonate it contains. The three categories are: dolomite (more than 40 percent magnesium carbonate); magnesium (between 5 and 40 percent magnesium carbonate) and calcite (less than 5 percent magnesium carbonate).

Marble was used for grave markers during the late 18th and throughout the 19th centuries, in all parts of the United States. Marble quarries are found in Vermont, Georgia, Alabama, and Colorado, with smaller quarries in Tennessee, Montana, and Texas. Marble was the most common grave marker material brought in from other places for use in early Iowa and the Midwest.

SLATE: This is a fine-grained stone that is formed from clay, shale, and sometimes quartz. It is formed in thin layers, is brittle, and is usually black, gray, or green. Slate commonly was used for 17th and 18th century grave markers in New England. Rarely was it used in Iowa and the Midwest.

CATLINITE: Although this stone is rarely used for grave markers, there are known examples of its use. It is often known as "pipestone," a very dense stone, and is brownish-red in color. The most famous quarries are now preserved in the Pipestone National Monument in Minnesota, although there were also quarries in Ontario, Canada.

IGNEOUS STONE

This type of stone is mainly formed from volcanic material such as magma. Beneath the earth's surface, liquid magma cooled and solidified. Mineral gases and liquids penetrated into the stone and created new crystalline formations with various colors.

GRANITE: Composed mainly of quartz, feldspar, and potassium. There are different types of granite depending upon the percentage of quartz, mica, and feldspar. Granite is a very hard material and is less likely to deteriorate through weathering and lichen growth than many other stones.

It mainly comes in darker colors, and contains very little calcite. Granite grave markers can be found in gray, red, pink, white, and black, as well as salmon-colored and variegated.

It was not until the Trow and Holden company in Vermont introduced the pneumatic carving hammer in 1890 that it became common to use granite for grave markers. Use of hand tools was simply too labor-intensive and time-consuming to be efficient or effective. After technology made it possible to shape and carve granite, it became the stone of choice for grave markers in the United States, because of its resistance to deterioration and damage. By the latter decades of the 19th century, granite became the most common choice for grave markers in Iowa and the Midwest.

The vast majority of grave markers sold in the United States in the 20th and 21st century are made from granite. The contemporary use of saws with diamond-edged blades, tungsten-carbide tipped tools, and carbon steel chisels now make the use of granite a much simpler matter. More recently there are high-definition laser techniques for creating images on the stone. Granite quarries are found in Connecticut, Georgia, North Carolina, Wisconsin, Minnesota, and many other states. Perhaps the most famous granite quarries are in the vicinity of Barre, Vermont.

Though granite is very hard and relatively impervious to weathering, it is not safe from staining. The most common stains sustained by granite grave markers include corrosion from metal ornamentation, salt crystallization, bird droppings, and gradual accumulation of dirt, smoke, soot, and acid in the air. Granite grave markers also are susceptible to graffiti, though the stone is so hard that it is difficult to vandalize.

OTHER STONES

Other types of stone were used in various areas of the United States but rarely are found in Iowa or the Midwest.

In some areas of New England and in New Jersey, a rock called Puddingstone was occasionally used to make grave markers. Mostly this substance is an Ediacaran, clast-supported pebble and cobble conglomerate. It is composed of grey feldspathic sand matrix and well-rounded small stones of quartzite, granite, felsite, and quartz monzonite. Because Puddingstone is a conglomerate, the stone itself is not conducive to the carving of inscriptions. Puddingstone grave markers usually consist of a boulder with a bronze plaque mounted on the stone.

In some regions of the United States grave markers also were made from **Fieldstone,** although rocks given this name are not the same geologic composition in all areas. The common definition of fieldstone is stone that is kept in its natural shapes, without any additional dressing other than incised inscriptions. Fieldstones often are simply glacial erratics. A fieldstone could be either metamorphic or igneous in origin; it is less likely that a fieldstone used as a grave marker would have been of a sedimentary type. As the name implies, fieldstones generally are recovered from the topsoil or subsoil rather than being quarried. Inscriptions carved on fieldstones ordinarily would have been incised lettering, but a very few examples of relief lettering survive.

PROCESSING THE STONE

The use of stone for making grave markers involves several steps. First the quarried stone has to be smoothed into a workable shape. This is called "dressing." Then the dressed stone has to be carved into the selected shape and the inscription or inscriptions carved on it.

There are six different ways of dressing stone.

1. **Hammer-dressed or quarry-faced surface.** This is the roughest form of surface finish. Stone removed from a quarry has large projections which need to be knocked off with a quarry hammer and then broken up into blocks of suitable size and shape.

2. **Rough-tooled surface.** In this type of surface the projections on the stone block are removed with chisels and the surface is smoothed down from its naturally rustic surface.

3. **Tooled surface.** Continuous parallel chisel marks throughout the surface of the stone. Different tooled surfaces are obtained by use of different sized chisels.

4. **Cut stone surface.** The surface is dressed by using a sharp chisel so that the chisel marks are nearly imperceptible. In the creation of grave markers, this surface is considered by most people to be superior to the tooled surface.

5. **Rubbed surface.** This finish is obtained by grinding or rubbing a cut stone surface by hand or machine until it is almost perfectly smooth.

6. **Polished surface.** Rubbed surfaces of limestone, marble, and granite are polished to enhance their textures. Polishing can be done by hand using sand and water or pumice. Or it can be done by a rubbing and polishing machine.

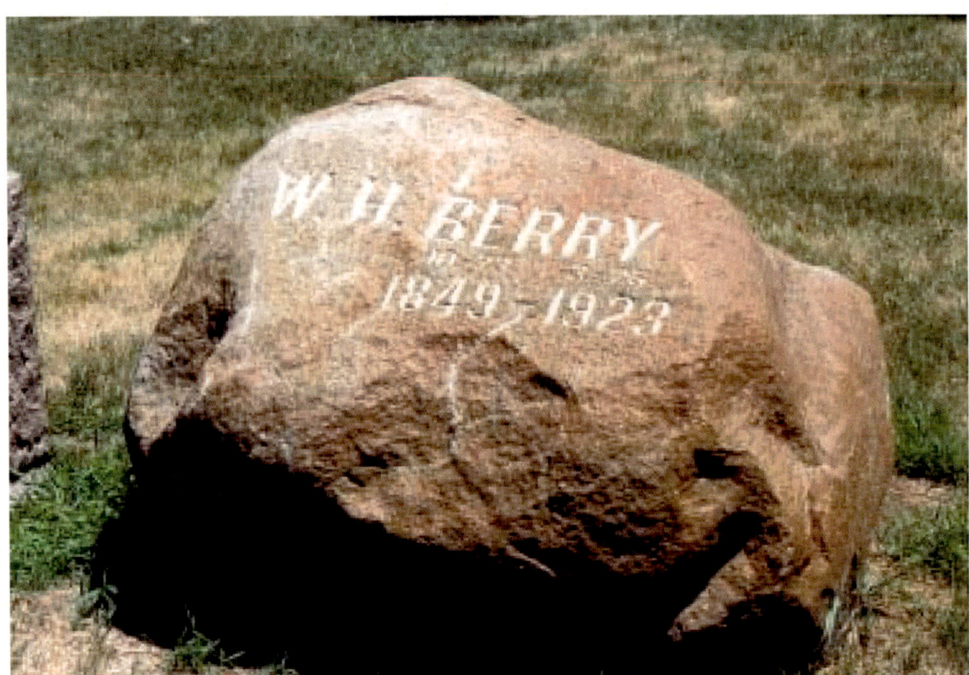

Regardless of the type of stone from which they are made, grave markers may have the cut stone surface, the rubbed surface, or the polished surface. There are some styles of grave markers which are artificially roughened, at least in part, to contrast with other parts of the same grave marker which has been carved in a design and then polished. In the advertisements of monument dealers, this design is called an "Emerging Stone."

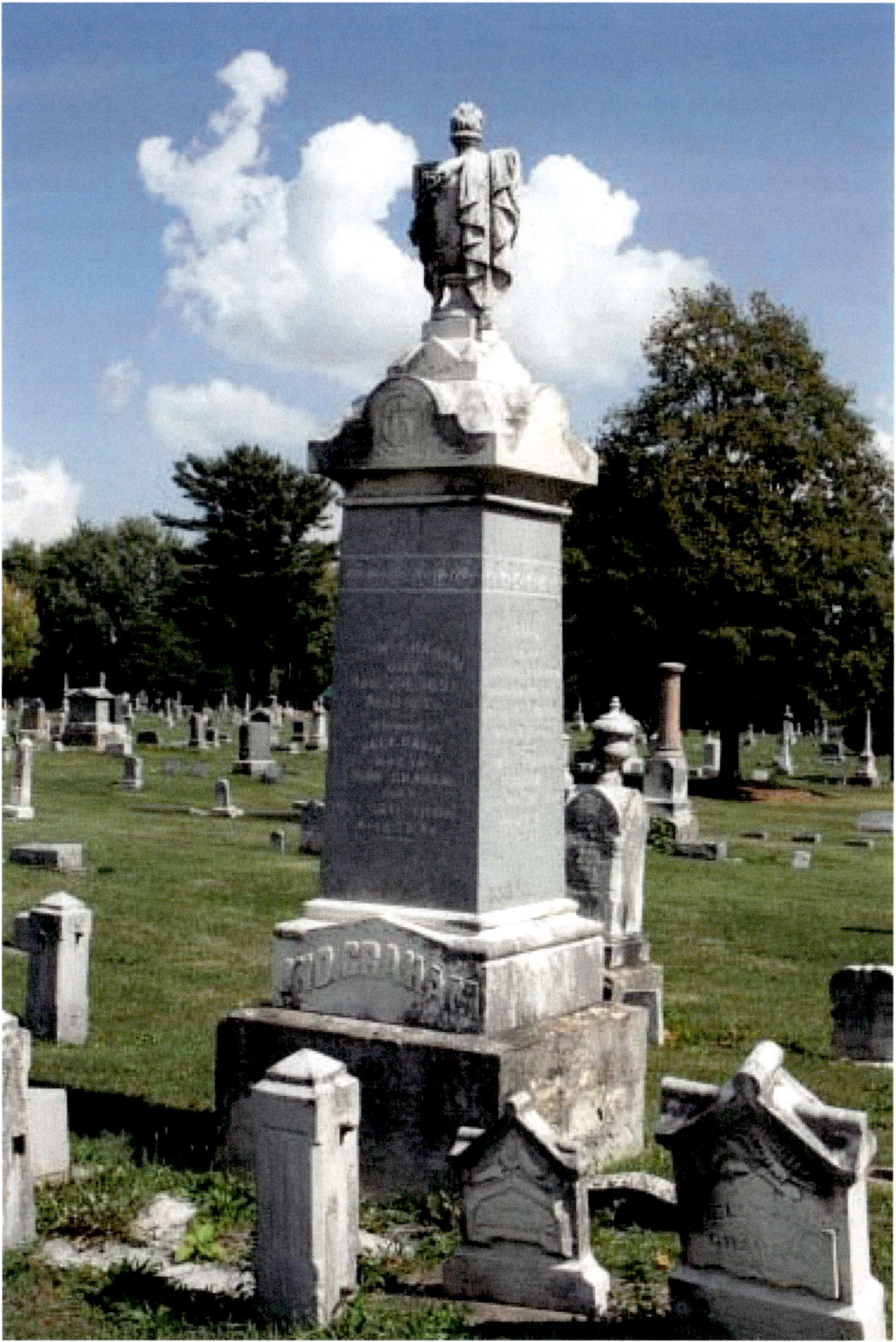

WHITE BRONZE GRAVE MARKERS

White bronze is a material used for grave markers from the 1870s until the first two decades of the 20th century. Though the trade name for the material is "white bronze," in reality the material is sand-blasted zinc. The original foundry was in Westport, Connecticut. Subsidiary foundries were established in Detroit, Michigan; Chicago, Illinois; and Des Moines, Iowa. White bronze grave markers are easily noted in cemeteries because they have a recognizable blue-gray color. Unless the grave marker was produced in the Westport foundry, the name of the foundry was cast on the smooth, slanted upper surface of the base of the marker. Similar white bronze grave markers were produced by the WZW Foundry in Warsaw, Missouri. Most white bronze grave markers had four sides, with a panel on each side which was bolted to the body of the monument. Each of the four panels contained information about the person or persons buried in the grave plot, or portrayed symbols.

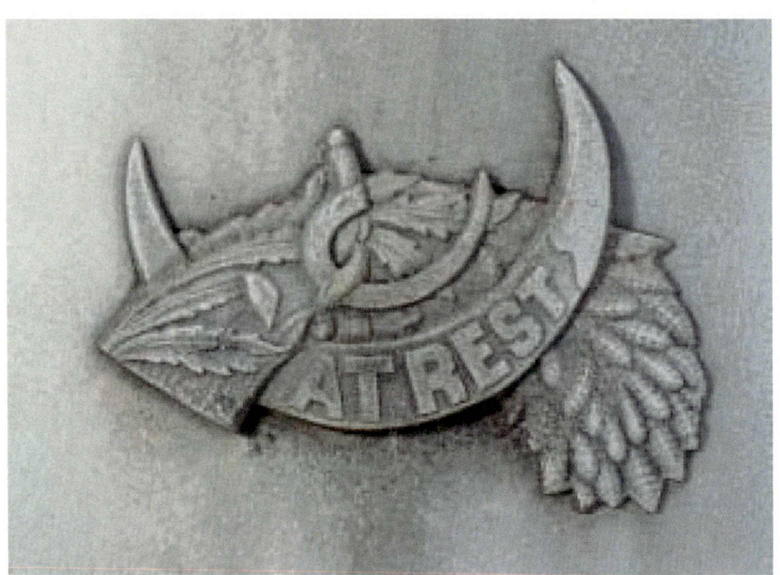

White bronze grave markers were cast hollow, and were of widely varying sizes and heights. There were dozens of designs of white bronze grave markers, including statuary. In some cases there was a family marker, and then individual markers added for each person buried on the lot. Some smaller markers simply indicated "mother," "father," or other family relationships.

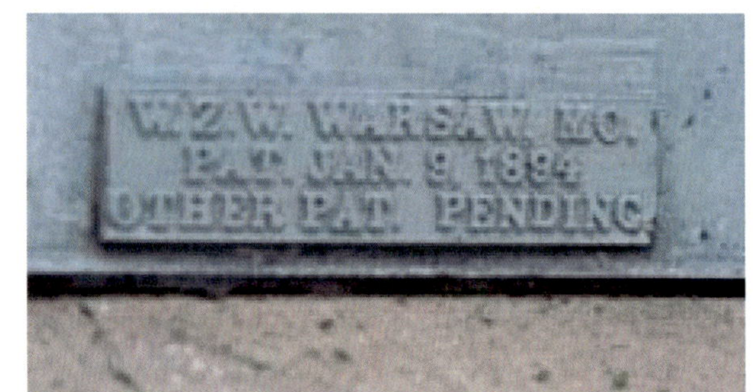

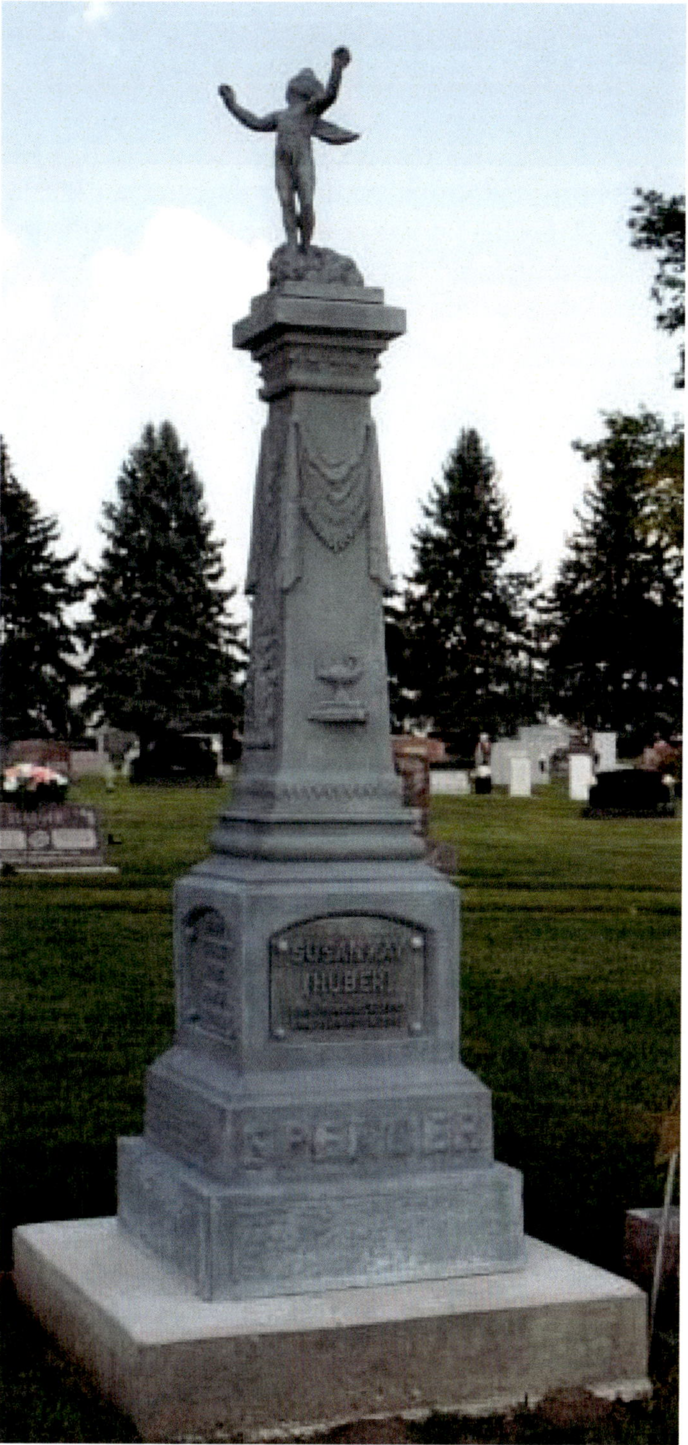

White bronze markers were priced on an equivalent scale with stone grave markers. Although the white bronze markers were very durable, some buckled at the base because of the excessive weight of the upper portions. White bronze markers fell out of favor because stone monument dealers argued that they would not last as long as stone markers. Many cemetery administrations did not allow white bronze markers to be erected. Only one known dealer, the Krebs Brothers of Cedar Rapids, Iowa, actually sold both stone and white bronze grave markers.

White bronze (sand-blasted zinc) also was used to cast many Civil War monuments, usually in the form of a uniformed soldier carrying a rifle. Such statues are found in city parks, on county court house lawns, and other public places throughout the northern states of the United States.

THE CAST IRON CROSSES OF CHARLES ANDERA

Charles (Karel) Andera was born in Bohemia (now Czech Republic), but with his parents and siblings, he emigrated to Canada in 1863, and then to Winneshiek County, Iowa. After his marriage to Barbara Dostal in 1875, he began work as a carpenter and wood carver, and later as the proprietor of a furniture store in Spillville, Iowa. Andera carved many items of church furniture which still exist in the Roman Catholic churches of the area. As a part of his furniture business he also built coffins.

In addition to his other activities, Charles Andera also designed and constructed cast iron grave marker crosses. The churchyard of St. Wenceslaus Church in Spillville contains dozens of examples of this phase of his work. He made patterns out of carved wood, and a foundry cast the crosses. When the finished crosses were returned to him, he trimmed, polished, and painted them. Although most of the Andera crosses which still exist are painted silver, Andera himself painted each one black with gold trim. Only a few examples of crosses in these original colors have been found, all in North Dakota.

Andera designed at least six different styles of crosses, and at least eleven different styles of the corpus figure. These crosses range in height from 5 feet 8 inches to 10 feet. They vary in weight from 108 to 318 pounds. Costs ranged from $10.50 to $47.00 each, and these prices were competitive with the more commonly found stone grave markers. Through advertisements in such publications as *The Catholic Workman*, people of Czech (Bohemian) descent all over the United States learned about these grave marker crosses and purchased them. Since Spillville never was on a railroad line, the crosses had to be carried by wagon (later by truck) from Andera's shop to the nearest railroad depot in Conover, 3½ miles away, for shipment. Andera grave marker crosses have been located in Iowa, Missouri, Minnesota, Texas, Oklahoma, Kansas, Nebraska, South Dakota, North Dakota, Wisconsin, Michigan, and New York.

Not only did Charles Andera design, finish, sell, and ship the grave marker crosses, he also devised a new formula for the molten iron from which they were cast. His formula was resistant to corrosion, which is one of the reasons so many of the crosses survive. The formula was analyzed by chemists and laboratories to determine the composition. The crosses were cast from molten iron mixed with a percentage of carbon, manganese, phosphorous, and silicon. The result not only produced very hard particles, but the molten iron had great fluidity, which allowed it to fill tiny crevices in delicate designs. Charles Andera cast iron grave marker crosses are both durable and beautiful. The majority of these crosses are found in grave yards near ethnic Bohemian (Czech) settlements, in Roman Catholic cemeteries, and occasionally in ethnically German Roman Catholic church yards.

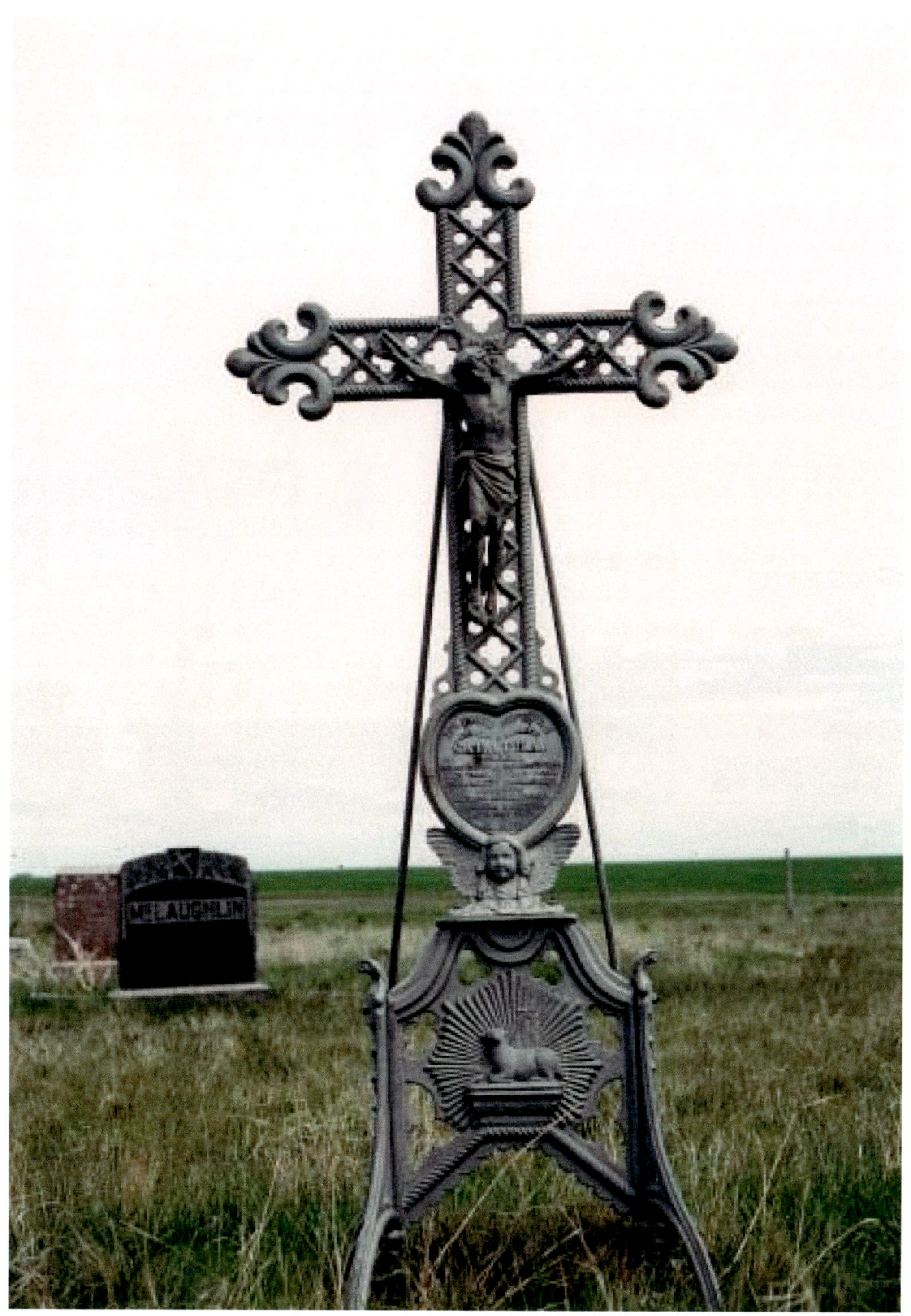
McLAUGHLIN

GLOSSARY

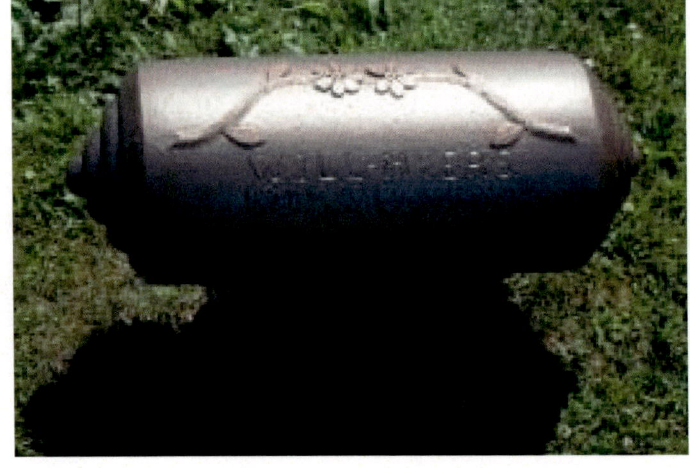

BOLSTER – The term used by monument dealers for the form of grave marker in which a cylinder rests on its side on a footing. There was a brief period in the late 19th and early 20th centuries when this type of grave marker was popular. Sometimes this style of grave markers is referred to as a "pillow" marker.

BURIAL VAULT – A container, also known as the burial liner, the grave vault, or grave liner. Its purpose was to prevent the weight of earth from collapsing the coffin beneath it. First made of wood, it later came to be made of brick, stone, concrete, or fiberglass. An early purpose was to prevent the sides of the grave from caving in before the burial took place.

BURYING GROUND – A tract of ground used predominantly for burial of human remains. Also commonly called Burial Ground. Term was most widely used in the 17th century.

CAIRN – A pile or stack of loose stones, that may or may not be mortared for stability. The word derives from the Gaelic *carn* and is used to describe things constructed by humans, never to refer to natural piles of stones. Cairns have been used throughout history for a variety of reasons, including marking burial sites, as memorials to the dead, as transportation markers, for ceremonial purposes, and many other purposes. Grave markers in the 19th and 20th centuries sometimes are imitations of cairns, but in those cases the stones almost always are mortared together. Some grave markers are carved out of one piece of stone, to look as if loose stones were mortared together.

CAPITAL -- Ornamention or decoration at the top of a column.

CASKET – Originally a casket was a small container in which jewels or other precious objects were kept. In more recent times the word has come to mean the container in which the corpse is placed before burial. A casket and a coffin are often confused and the words often are used interchangeably. When used for funeral purposes, a casket is a different design and shape than a coffin. The word first became associated with funerals as a euphemism within the undertakers' profession. For general definition purposes, a casket is a rectangular box, often with a divided lid which is hinged, and with attached handles. A casket ordinarily is lined with cloth. A casket is usually constructed of wood or of metal, although other materials might be used.

CATACOMB - An underground cemetery, especially one consisting of tunnels and rooms with recesses to contain coffins. The word catacomb derives from the Late Latin *catacumbae* which probably was a corruption of an earlier Latin phrase *cata tumbas*, meaning "among the tombs." Catacombs necessarily are subterranean chambers containing corpses and coffins.

CEMETERY - Contemporary meaning is the same as burying ground or grave yard. The term came into common use in the 19th century. The word derives from the Greek *koimeterion*, which means "sleeping place or dormitory." After the Greek, the Latin *coimeterium* and the Old French *cimetiere* are the roots, and both mean "grave yard." The original Greek roots are *koiman*, meaning "to put to sleep," and *keimai*, meaning "I lie down."

CENOTAPH - An empty tomb, or a monument erected to honor a person who is buried elsewhere. Also, it can mean the original burial place for a corpse which has been moved elsewhere. The word derives from two Greek roots: *kenos* meaning "empty" and *taphos* meaning "a burial, a place for a burial, or a grave."

CHARNEL HOUSE - A building or chamber in which corpses or bones are deposited. The phrase derives from the Latin *carn* or *caro*, meaning "flesh." From that the phrase became *carnarium* in Medieval Latin, and *carnel* or *charnel* in Anglo-French and Middle English. A charnel house is where human skeletal remains are stored, sometimes after the bones have been uncovered from burial places in a cemetery.

CHRISTOGRAM - The monogram I.H.S. or IHS is a symbol of Jesus. The letters are the Anglicization of the first letters of the word Jesus in Greek. The monogram is commonly used on grave markers.

CHURCH YARD - Originally this meant the area surrounding a church. Parts of the area were used for burial purposes. In Christian tradition, this meant it was consecrated ground. Burial in proximity to the church building was a high honor. The closer to the church building, the higher the honor. The north (shady) side of the church building was the least respected part of the church yard. To be buried on the north side of the church building was an indication of low status.

COFFIN – A container for the corpse, during the funeral, and for burial, usually made of wood. The word derives from the Latin *cophinus* which means "cradle." This in turn was derived from the Greek *kophinos* which means "basket." In Old French the word became *cofin,* from which the English "coffin" comes. A coffin originally was hexagonal in shape, flared at the top end and narrowed at the bottom end. This shape symbolically conformed to the shape of a human body. The idea was that a person's shoulders are wider than their feet. Originally a coffin had a removable lid, which was sealed shut in place by screws at the time of burial. Most early coffins did not have attached handles and were carried by means of poles under them, or by placing them on men's shoulders. It was common to have metal plates affixed to the lids of coffins before burial, as a means of respect and also a means of identification of the person buried in that particular coffin. Most metal plates were removed prior to burial. This sort of coffin furniture was sold separately from the coffin. It also was possible to buy coffin handles, which were detached prior to the burial.

COLUMBARIUM – A place for the storage of funerary urns. The word derives from the Latin *columba,* which means "dove." The term originally referred to compartmentalized housing for doves, called a dovecote. Contemporary columbaria can be free-standing or built into the walls of existing churches or other structures.

CREMAINS – The term used to refer to the ashes of a cremated corpse.

CREMATION – The process of reducing a corpse to ashes. This process usually is carried out in a crematorium. The ashes may then be pulverized and placed in an urn or otherwise disposed of.

CROSS -- Because there are so many variations of crosses, a special section has been devoted to them. (See pages 71-77)

CRYPT – A crypt is a stone or masonry chamber beneath the floor of a church or other structure. The word derives from the Latin *crypta,* which means "vault." A crypt may contain coffins, sarcophagi, or religious relics.

EMERGING STONE – A type of grave marker where one portion of the stone has been fully carved, or dressed, while another portion remains undressed or only partially dressed or smoothed. This gives the impression of a stone that has been incompletely carved, or partially left as it came from the quarry. Actually the undressed portion of the grave marker has been artificially roughened. This style of grave marker was popular during the late 19th and early 20th century, when it was supposed to represent a life partially completed but cut short. Almost invariably the "Emerging Stone" is of granite.

EPITAPH – An epitaph may be an inscription on a grave marker or a tomb, and usually consists of words identifying or in memory of the deceased person buried or entombed there. An epitaph also may be a brief statement commemorating the positive qualities of a deceased person. On occasion the word may be used in place of "eulogy."

EXHUMATION -- To remove remains from a grave or tomb.

FUNERAL – A formal ceremony or liturgical service held after a death, and before the burial of the corpse.

GARDEN CEMETERY – Often used synonymously with "Rural Cemetery." The term came into use during the early 19th century in the United States to describe cemeteries on the outskirts of cities, and cemeteries which were landscaped and park-like. Mount Auburn Cemetery in Cambridge, Massachusetts is considered to be the first Garden Cemetery or Rural Cemetery in the United States. Mount Auburn was platted in 1831 and sometimes was referred to as a "Garden of Graves." The landscape design included flowers, shrubs, trees, sculptures, impoundments of water, and curved walkways and driveways. It was common during the 19th century for families to have picnics on or near the plots where family members were buried.

GRAVE – A grave is a location where a corpse has been buried *beneath the surface of the ground*. Cremated remains also may be buried in graves. Graves usually are marked with an identification of who is buried there, although not all grave markers are made of permanent materials. Graves are to be found in burying grounds, grave yards, church yards, and cemeteries.

GRAVE MARKER – Any object or device which identifies and/or describes the person whose corpse is buried in a particular grave.

GRAVE STONE – A marker made of stone which identifies and/or describes the person whose corpse is buried in a particular grave.

GRAVE YARD – A tract of ground used predominantly for burial of human remains.

HOLDING VAULT – Another term for the "Receiving Vault" or "Public Vault." It was a structure used to store a corpse when the ground was frozen too hard to dig a grave. Also, in times of epidemics or mass tragedies, the number of corpses might be more than could be buried simultaneously. The holding vault was a place of temporary storage until the corpses could be handled with safety or with respect.

INCISED LETTERING – Letters that are carved into the surface of the grave marker. The expression means to cut into, to carve into, or to engrave by cutting into the surface of the stone or wood to create words, symbols, or other designs.

I.H.S. or IHS – See "Christogram."

INHUMATION – The practice of disposing of corpses by burying them in the ground. An inhumation may be in a grave, in a trench, in a barrow, in a natural cave, or in other natural geological features. The term also can be used when the corpse is laid on the surface of the ground and then covered with heaped-up earth or with stones. The depth of the inhumation does not alter the definition.

INTERMENT – Burial in the ground. Alternate term for "inhumation."

INURNMENT – The placement of cremated remains in an urn. Usually the meaning includes the placing of the urn in a niche or other place of final disposition.

LEDGER MARKER – See "Slab Marker."

LICHEN -- A complex organism made up of an algae and a fungus in a symbiotic relationship. Lichens often grow on stone surfaces and can cause slow deterioration of the stone. Lichens are often mistakenly referred to as moss.

LITHIC – Usually used as a prefix or as a suffix. It derives from the Greek word *lithos* or *lithikos*, meaning "made of or pertaining to stone." As a suffix it is found in such words as Paleolithic, meaning old stone age, or Neolithic, meaning new stone age. Lithology is the study of rocks and stones. In regard to grave markers, a Monolith is a single stone and a Megalith is a large stone. Although recent grave markers are rarely referred to in these terms, they are appropriate when a modern grave marker is particularly large, or when it stands alone and not surrounded by other grave markers. See "Cairn."

LYCH GATE – A covered gateway, usually at the entrance to a Church Yard. The name derives from the Saxon word *lych,* meaning "corpse." In Anglican churchyards, it was traditionally a place where corpse-bearers paused between funeral and burial. The corpse was laid on a bier in the lych gate and the officiant began the first part of the burial liturgy there. Lych gates usually are made of wood, although there are examples which are made of brick and of stone. They may be roofed with wood, thatch, or clay tiles, or even on occasion with corrugated iron. Lych gates are most common in the British Isles.

MAUSOLEUM – A free-standing building constructed solely as a monument to the deceased, and containing burial chambers for one or more coffins. Often a mausoleum is called a tomb, and the reverse is also true. The word derives from the grave of King Mausolus, Persian Satrap of Caria, at Halicarnassus. Perhaps the most famous mausoleum in the world is the Taj Mahal in Agra, India.

MEMENTO MORI – A Latin expression which means "Remember that you have to die." It was part of a common statement when a Roman general came back victorious from a battle. During his triumphal parade, a slave was ordered to say: *"Respice post te. Hominem te memento,"* translated as "Look after you to the time after your death and remember you are only a man." The purpose was to avoid the risk of becoming haughty and having delusions of grandeur. During the Middle Ages in Europe it became an important part of *"ars moriendi,"* or "The Art of Dying." The expression also is used as a term for the roadside memorials which mark the site of deaths from automobile accidents.

MONUMENT – A physical object which commemorates the death of or the burial of a person. Common monuments are grave markers, mausoleums, stela, and tombs.

NECROPOLIS – In ancient times the term meant a large cemetery with many elaborate tombs and monuments. The word is from the Greek *necropolis,* which means "City of the Dead."

OOLITIC LIMESTONE – A geological feature which occurs in abundance in and around Bedford, Indiana. It is one of the best-known of building stones in the United States. Oolitic limestone is soft and easily worked, but at the same time it is durable and strong. According to geological reports, it is more easily cut and carved than any other well-known building stone, and it will retain the carving in good preservation longer than any other stone of equal softness. Although oolitic limestone is relatively soft and easy to carve when it is quarried, with exposure to the air it hardens as the moisture dissipates. Grave markers made of oolitic limestone are found in many Midwestern cemeteries. They can easily be recognized because they often take the form of tree stumps or tree trunks. These grave markers were offered to members of the Woodmen of the World and Modern Woodmen of America during the last half of the 19th century and the early 20th century.

OSSUARY – A container or room in which human bones are placed or stored. The word derives from Latin *oss* meaning "bone" and *arius* meaning of or related to," and developed into Late Latin *ossuarium*. An ossuary may be a receptacle or a structure. Ossuaries frequently were created where burial space was scarce. A body was first buried in a temporary grave. After a period of years the skeletal remains were excavated and removed to an ossuary. The original grave site then could be used again, a process often called "renewal". It is possible to store the remains of many more bodies in a single receptacle than if the original coffins were left intact.

POTTER'S FIELD – A part of the cemetery set aside for the burials of persons deemed unsuitable for burial in the regular sections. Potter's Fields were places for burial of any person who was rejected by the social units of the community, for any reason. This group included such people as paupers, the indigent, strangers, suicides, and those executed for crimes. It also might include unidentified accident victims who died in the area, and those who died as inmates or residents of government institutions. When families did not claim such bodies, they often were buried in Potter's Fields. Sometimes the Potter's Field was located at the north edge of a cemetery. Sometimes it was located outside the fence or wall of the cemetery. Sometimes it was a separate area altogether. The purpose was to create an obvious segregation of these corpses from those who were buried in family plots, or from those who purchased their own gravesites. The name comes from The Bible, Matthew, 27: 7: "After conferring together, they (the chief priests and elders) used them to buy the potter's field as a place to bury foreigners." This refers to the suicide of Judas after he returned the thirty pieces of silver, and the method to be used in spending the returned thirty pieces of silver.

PUBLIC VAULT - See "Holding Vault."

RAISED LETTERING – See "Relief Lettering."

RECEIVING VAULT – See "Holding Vault."

RELIEF LETTERING –Lettering on the grave marker in which the letters are carved so they are raised above the surface or background of the base material. "Raised lettering" often refers only to the words and numbers on the grave marker. "Relief lettering" may also refer to the symbols and sculptural figures which appear on the grave marker. Relief carving was more difficult and therefore was more expensive.

R.I.P. or RIP – Derived from the Latin *Requiescat in pace,* meaning "Rest in peace." RIP is an abbreviation which expresses wishes for eternal rest and peace for a deceased person. Early in the Christian era a more common expression was *dormit in pace,* meaning "He sleeps in peace." By the 18th century the initials became very common on grave markers, particularly for Roman Catholic and Anglican deaths, but other Christian denominations also use "RIP."

ROUGH BOX – See "Burial Vault." The term rough box was appropriate when the liner for the grave was made of wood. The inside of the liner was smoothed to allow the easy lowering of the coffin. The outside of the box, which was against the earth, remained rough and unfinished, because no one saw it. In contemporary times, the rough box has been supplanted by the concrete vault. The purpose of the two objects is substantially the same. In the cases of rough boxes and vaults, one of the main purposes was to keep the sides of the grave from caving in prior to the burial and to keep the weight of the earth on top of the grave from collapsing the coffin.

RURAL CEMETERY – See "Garden Cemetery." Although the two terms are often used inter-changeably, a "Rural Cemetery" by definition was outside the city limits. A "Garden Cemetery" might be located within the city limits. The landscape design was the same. It is a proper noun expression and does not mean any small cemetery in a rural area.

RUSTICATION – The artificial roughening of the edges of a stone grave marker. Some designs used this technique to create the impression that the grave marker remained as it was first quarried. There are many examples of rusticated grave stones which have classical sculpture portions on one side and roughened portions on the opposite side. Rustication was a fashion in the late 19th and early 20th centuries.

SARCOPHAGUS – (plural, Sarcophagi) A box-like receptacle for a corpse. A sarcophagus commonly is made of stone. The word derives from the Greek *sarx* meaning "flesh" and *phagein* meaning "to eat." The full Greek expression was *lithos sarcophagus,* meaning "flesh-eating stone." Apparently it originally referred to a particular type of limestone that was thought to speed the process of decomposition. Most sarcophagi were designed to remain above ground level.

SEPULCHRE – A term used indiscriminately to describe a grave, a mausoleum, a sarcophagus, a tomb, a vault, or a burial place. The word derives from the Latin *sepelire* or *sepulcrum* which mean "to bury." The more recent derivation is from Old French *sepulcre*, meaning the same thing.

SLAB MARKER – This is a slab of stone that covers the entire length and width of the grave. It might be the actual grave marker, or it might be in addition to another style of grave marker placed at the head of the grave. Slab markers also are called "ledger markers" or "full ledgers."

STELE or STELA – A carved or inscribed stone slab or pillar used for commemorative purposes. The word derives from Greek *stellein*, which means "to set up" or "to make stand," through the Latin *stela* and Old High German *stollo*, meaning a "pillar."

SYMBOL – A symbol is a mark, sign, picture, or word that indicates, signifies, or is understood as representing an idea, an object, or a relationship. Symbols allow people to go beyond what is known or seen, by creating linkages between otherwise very different concepts and experiences. The word derives from Greek *symbolon*, meaning "token" or "watchword." It is an amalgam of *syn* which means "together" and *bole*, "a throwing or casting." Apparently over much time the meaning has shifted, from "throwing things together" to "comparisons." It now means an outward and visible sign of some object or idea – a symbol is something which stands for something else. For purposes of this glossary, symbols are visual signs that have both a literal meaning and also stand for another more metaphorical meaning.

TOMB – A grave, a place of burial, a vault, a chamber containing a corpse, or a monument commemorating a deceased person. The derivation of the word is from the Greek *tumbos*, meaning "burial mound," the Late Latin *tumba*, which also means "burial mound," and from Old French *tombe*, with exactly the same meaning.

TOMB STONE – Literally a "tomb stone" is the tablet on the side of a tomb which either identifies the person entombed within, or contains an elegy to that person.

For purposes of our glossary, a tomb is an above-ground disposal of a corpse. Therefore, if the corpse is buried beneath the surface of the ground, it is in a grave and cannot be marked with a tomb stone. This glossary makes a definite distinction between a "grave marker," which marks a *below the ground* disposal of a corpse, and a "tomb stone," which identifies an *above the ground* disposal of a corpse.

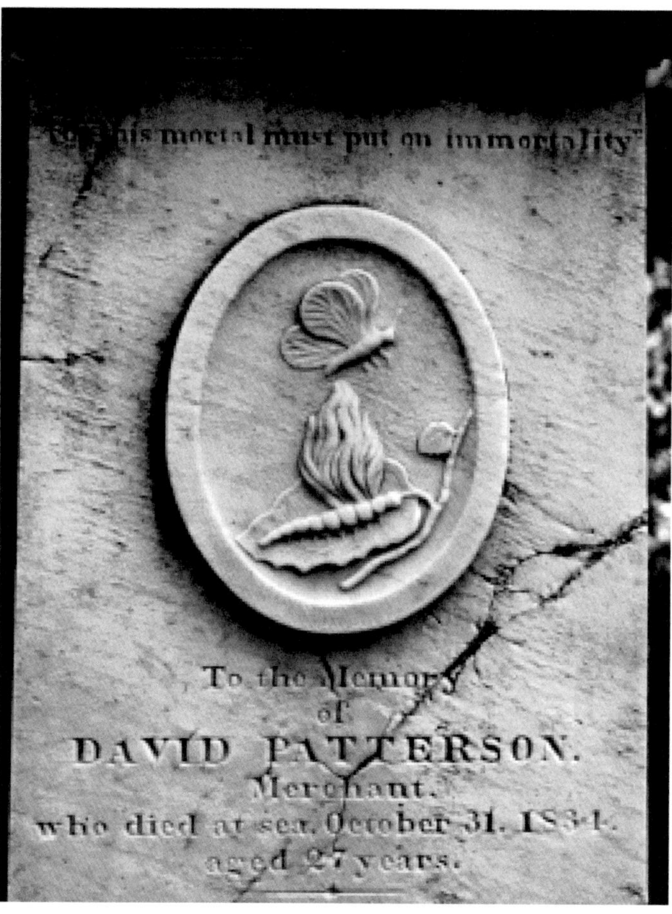

TUMULUS – (plural, Tumuli) A mound of earth and stones raised over a grave. Such mounds also are known as "barrows" or "kurgans." Present "cairns" may originally have been "tumuli" and over time the earth has been worn away, leaving only stones. There are various kinds of barrows. The word derives from Latin meaning "mound" or "small hill." Originally the word may have come from an Indo-European root *teuh*, meaning "to bulge" or "to swell."

URN – A vase, often with a cover, that usually has a narrow neck above a rounded body. Since prehistoric times, each culture and civilization throughout the world has used urns for many purposes, not only as burial vessels. There are instances where body parts were placed in urns, especially the heart, but in this glossary we are concerned only with funerary urns used to contain cremains. Both funerary urns and cinerary urns may be burial urns, containing the cremated remains of deceased persons.

VAULT – See "Burial Vault" and "Receiving Vault."

PRICE TWO GUINEAS.

THE SCULPTOR'S

AND

CEMETERY MASON'S

PORTFOLIO OF DESIGNS,

FOR

Monuments, Tombs, Crosses, Headstones, Chimney Pieces, Borders to Graves, Garden Vases, Drinking Fountains, Pedestals for Sun Dials, &c.,

WITH DETAILED PLANS.

BY

JOSEPH BARLOW ROBINSON,

SCULPTOR, DERBY,

Author of the following works, "Designs for Monuments," "Cemetery and Churchyard Memorials," "Epitaphs from the Cemeteries of the United Kingdom," "In Memoriam," "Trade Secrets," "Designs for Alphabets," "Carved Panels," "Architectural Foliage," &c.

PUBLISHED BY THE AUTHOR,

AND MAY BE HAD FROM HIM, OR HIS TRAVELLING AGENTS IN THE UNITED KINGDOM, ALSO FROM HIS AGENTS IN PARIS, BRUSSELS, NEW YORK, AND SYDNEY, NEW SOUTH WALES.

BIBLIOGRAPHY

19th-CENTURY RESOURCES

BOOKS BY JOSEPH BARLOW ROBINSON:

In Remembrance: A Series of Designs for Monuments, Tombs, Gravestones, &c. (1855)

Gothic Ornaments Adapted from Nature. (1857)

Cemetery and Churchyard Memorials. (1857)

Memorials, Original and Selected: A Series of Nearly One Hundred Designs for Memorials, Tombs, Tablets, Gravestones, Panels, Scrolls, Alphabets, &c &c with Plans and Details. (1859)

Trade Secrets: A Collection of Practical Receipts for the Use of Sculptors, Modellers, Stone Masons, Builders, Marble Masons, Polishers, &c to Which is Added a Description of the Various Stones in the United Kingdom Suitable for Monumental Purposes &c. (1862)

Cemetery and Churchyard Memorials. (1862)

Designs for Gravestones, Crosses, &c. (1865)

The Cemetery Mason's Useful Book of Designs for Headstones, Crosses, Alphabets, &c. (1868)

Designs for Monuments. (nd)

The Sculptor's and Cemetery Mason's Portfolio of Designs. (nd)

BOOKS BY JOHN ROMILLY ALLEN:

Notes on Early Christian Symbolism. London: G. Bell & Sons, 1884.

Early Christian Symbolism in Great Britain and Ireland Before the Thirteenth Century: The Rhind Lectures in Archaeology for 1885. London: Whiting & Company, 1887.

Old Cornish Crosses. Truro: J. Pollard, 1896.

The Early Christian Monuments of Scotland: A Classified, Illustrated, Descriptive List of the Monuments, with an Analysis of the Symbolism and Ornamentation. Edinburgh: Neill & Company, 1903. (2 volumes)

Celtic Art in Pagan and Christian Times. London: Methuen & Company, 1904.

OTHER 19TH CENTURY BOOKS ABOUT SYMBOLISM

J. W. Hallam, *Monumental Memorials: Designs for Headstones and Mural Monuments.* London: Joseph Masters, 1858.

William Palmer, *An Introduction to Early Christian Symbolism: Being the Description of a Series of Fourteen Compositions, from Fresco-Paintings, Glasses, and Carcophagi, with Three Appendices.* London: Longman, Green, Longman and Roberts, 1859.

William and George Audsley, *Handbook of Christian Symbolism.* London: Day & Son, Limited, 1865.

Floral Album and Ladies' Companion. New Haven: C. G. Clark & Company, 1867.

Floral Hand Book. Boston: Joseph Burnett & Company, 1876.

Frederick Edward Hulme, *The History, Principles, and Practice of Symbolism in Christian Art.* London: Swan, Sonnenschein & Company, 1892.

The books listed above would have been available to stone carvers and monument dealers in the United States during the latter half of the 19th century.

Obviously not all of these books are references for the symbols on grave markers. But 19th-century stone carvers often considered themselves to be artists, and during their apprenticeships they would very likely have come into contact with pattern books and guide books for the craft. Books explaining the language of flowers were very common, and often were included in the almanacs of the time. Almanacs were found in almost every home and therefore the language of flowers would have been well-known to everyone, stone carvers included. While we cannot be absolutely sure that the stone carvers and monument dealers in the United States, especially in the Midwest region, had access to guidebooks about symbols, it is plausible that they did. Books about the meanings of symbols would not have been published if no one purchased them. Just like the plethora of etiquette books published in the latter half of the 19th century, the very quantity gives some assurance that people purchased them, and we may have some presumption that these books, if not read, were often referred to.

MONUMENTAL MEMORIALS:

BEING

DESIGNS

FOR

Headstones and Mural Monuments.

PART II.

BY

J. W. HALLAM, ARCHITECT.

LONDON:
JOSEPH MASTERS, ALDERSGATE STREET,
AND NEW BOND STREET.
MDCCCLVIII.

CEMETERY SYMBOLS WORKSHEET

Symbol	Where found	Cemetery	Date found/ date on stone	Notes

ABOUT THE AUTHORS

LOREN N. HORTON was born in Iowa and has lived in the state most of his life. He traces his first Iowa ancestor to 1838. Horton received the B.A. and M.A. degrees from Iowa State Teachers College (now University of Northern Iowa), and the Ph.D. degree from The University of Iowa. He was a teacher in Iowa secondary schools and at the junior college level, and was employed by the State Historical Society of Iowa for 24 years, retiring as Senior Historian. Horton also has served as adjunct instructor at Iowa Wesleyan College and The University of Iowa. He is the author of several books and numerous magazine articles.

MICHAEL D. ZAHS is part of a nine-generation Iowa family and grew up on a century farm near Haskins. He is the fourth generation of his family to attend the same one-room school. Zahs is the last person to graduate from high school in Ainsworth. He received degrees in biology from the University of Northern Iowa in 1969 and 1971. Zahs taught junior high students science and social studies for 39 years. He has taken care of cemeteries since 1964. Zahs's hobbies are cemeteries, Iowa history, collecting buildings, and the Brinton Collection. He and his wife, Julie, have adult children, Hannah and Adam.

Zahs and Horton began working together in 1987 with the *Iowa: Eye To I* tours (graduate level courses) from Iowa Wesleyan College. The program was organized into seven different tours, some of them travelling as much as 2,000 miles within Iowa. These classes were taught on a bus as the participants toured to places of interest and importance. The two men also participated in the Iowa Sesquicentennial Celebration, sponsored by the Smithsonian Institution on the Mall in Washington, D.C., and which was repeated on the State Capitol grounds in Des Moines. These festivals were patterned after the *Iowa: Eye To I* tours. They also have led many other tours of Iowa and adjacent states. On their travels together they enjoy stopping at cemeteries, as an introduction to learning about the communities.

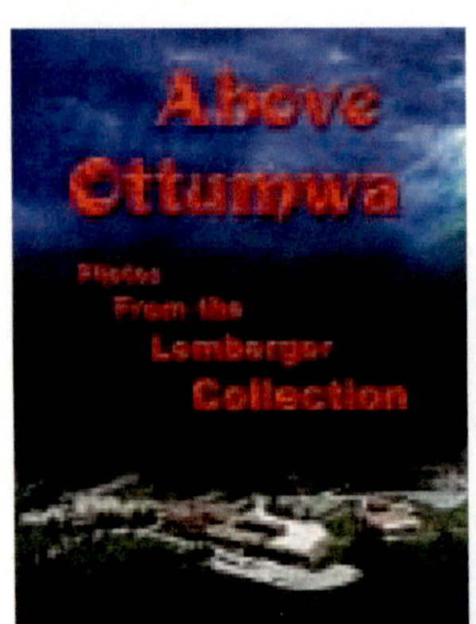
Above
Ottumwa
Photos
From the
Lemberger
Collection
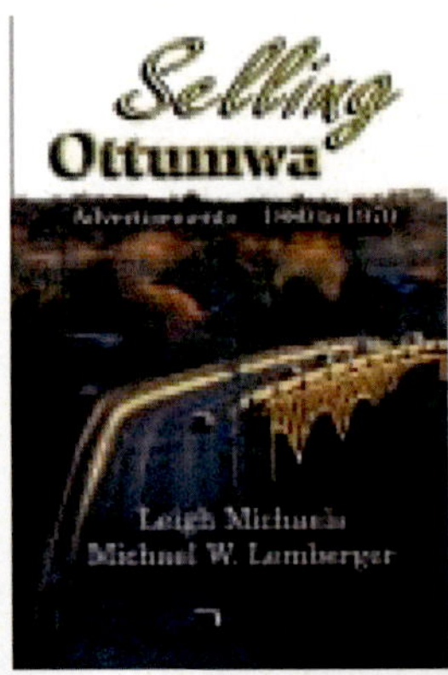
Selling
Ottumwa
Leigh Michaels
Michael W. Lemberger
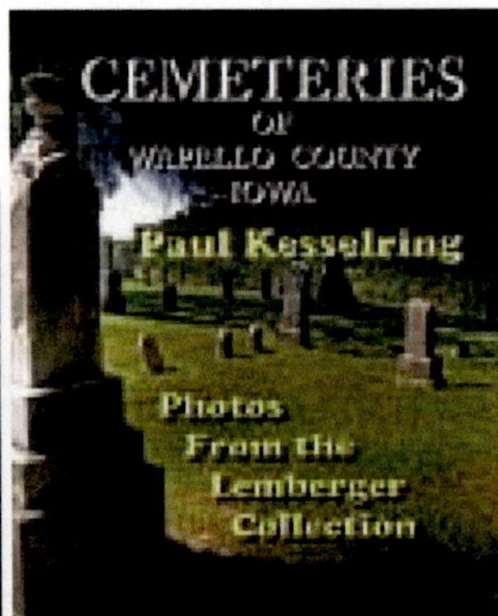
CEMETERIES
OF
WAPELLO COUNTY
IOWA
Paul Kesselring
Photos
From the
Lemberger
Collection
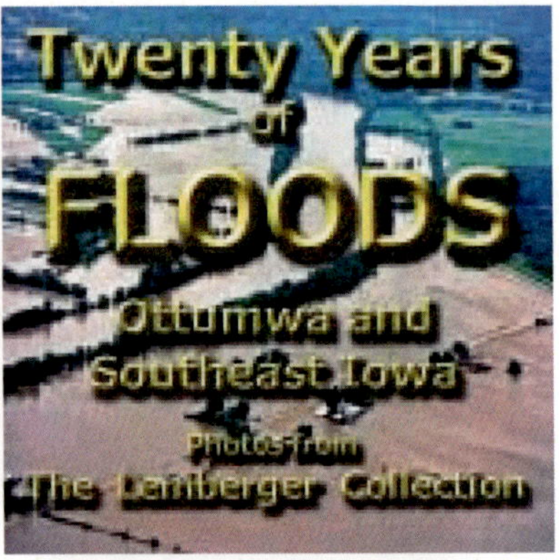
Twenty Years
of
FLOODS
Ottumwa and
Southeast Iowa
Photos from
The Lemberger Collection
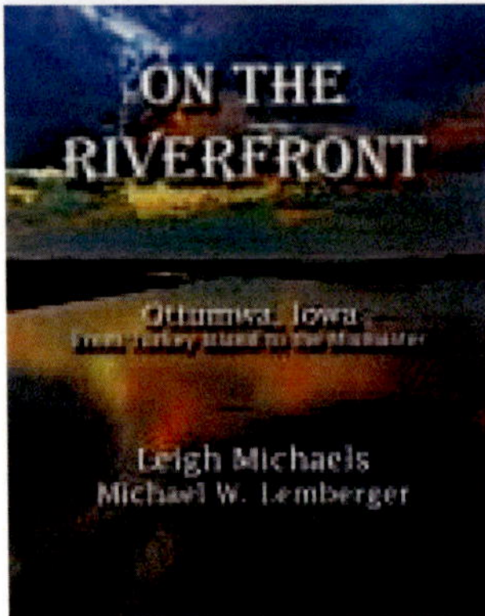
ON THE
RIVERFRONT
Ottumwa, Iowa
Leigh Michaels
Michael W. Lemberger
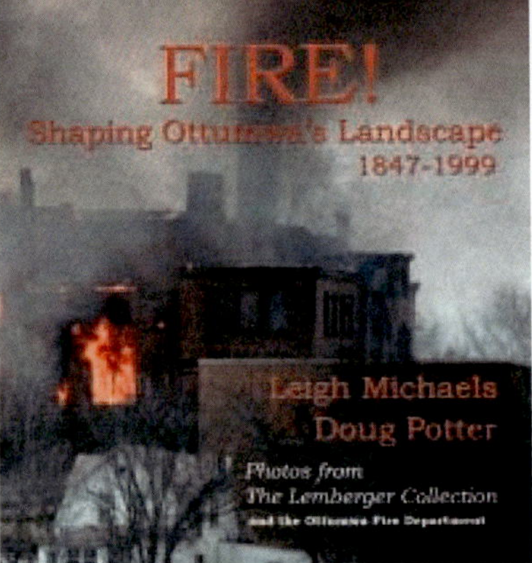
FIRE!
Shaping Ottumwa's Landscape
1847-1999
Leigh Michaels
Doug Potter
Photos from
The Lemberger Collection
and the Ottumwa Fire Department
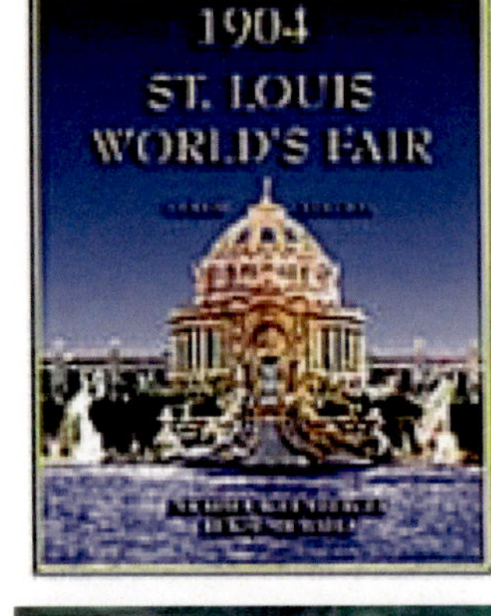
1904
ST. LOUIS
WORLD'S FAIR
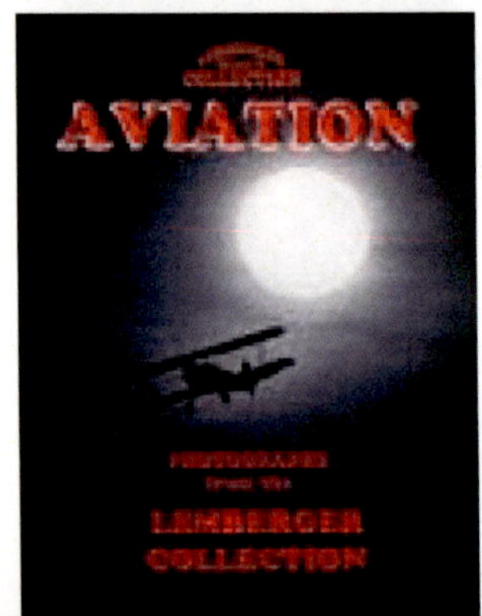
AVIATION
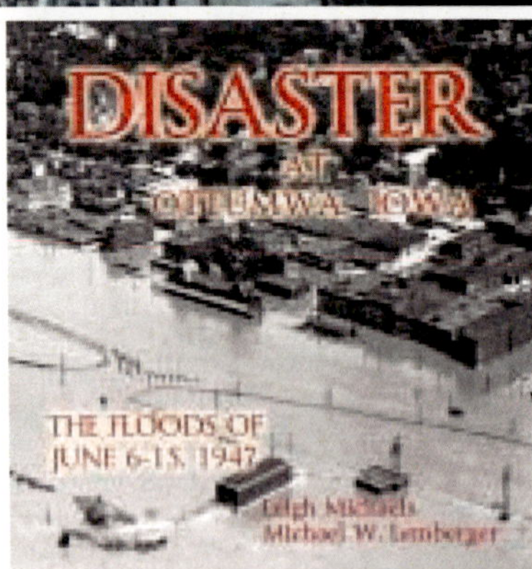
DISASTER
AT
OTTUMWA, IOWA
THE FLOODS OF
JUNE 6-15, 1947
Leigh Michaels
Michael W. Lemberger
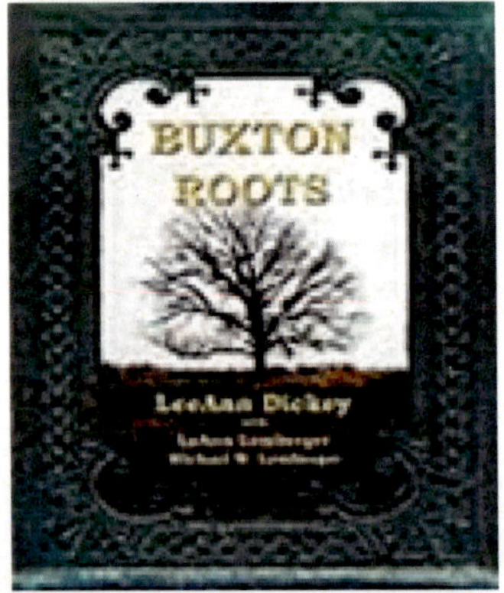
BUXTON
ROOTS
LeeAnn Dickey
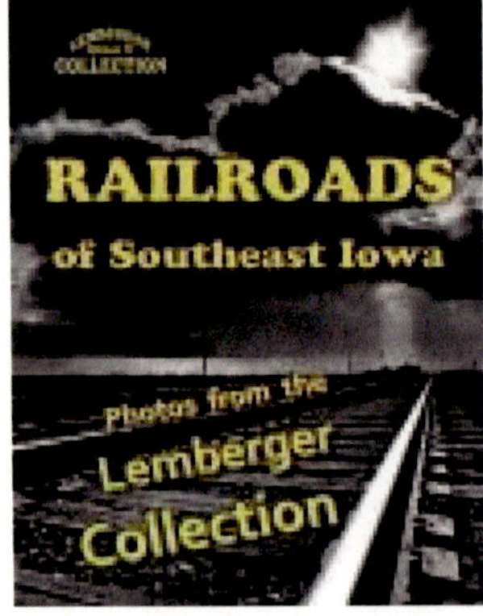
RAILROADS
of Southeast Iowa
Photos from the
Lemberger
Collection
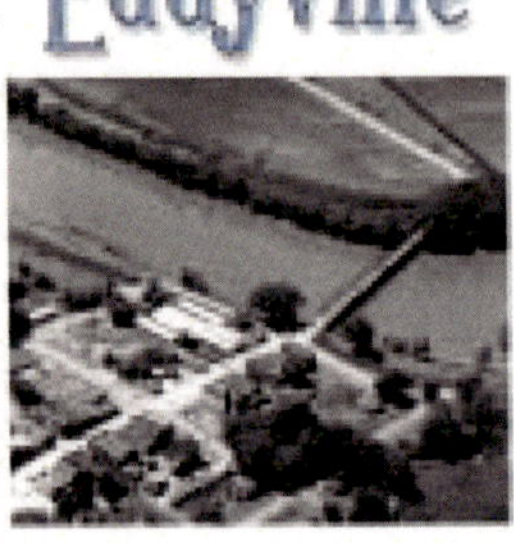
Eddyville
Lee Ann Sammers Dickey
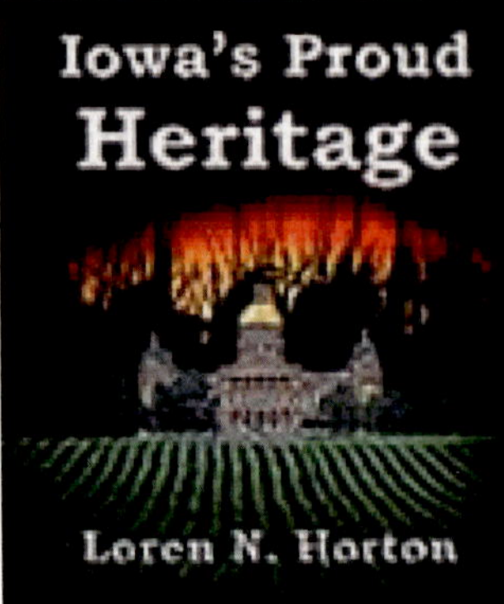
Iowa's Proud
Heritage
Loren N. Horton
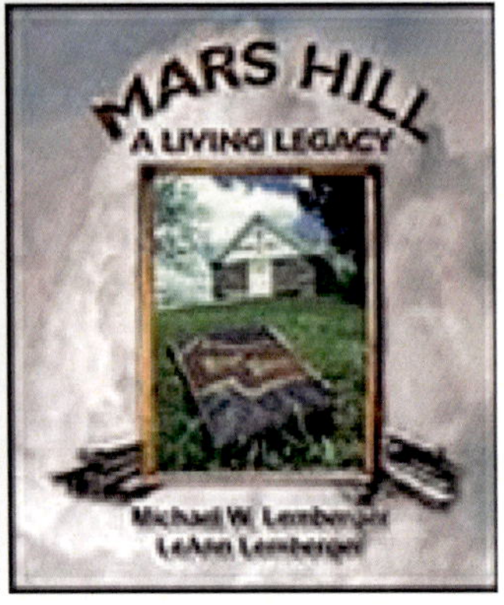
MARS HILL
A LIVING LEGACY
Michael W. Lemberger
LeAnn Lemberger

Made in the USA
San Bernardino, CA
01 March 2018